Teachers as
Cultural Workers

Teachers as Cultural Workers

Letters to Those Who Dare Teach

PAULO FREIRE

*translated by Donaldo Macedo, Dale Koike,
and Alexandre Oliveira*

*with a foreword by Donaldo Macedo
and Ana Maria Araújo Freire*

Westview Press
A Member of the Perseus Books Group

Copyright © 2005 by Paulo Freire
Published by Westview Press,
A Member of the Perseus Books Group

Westview Press books are available at special discounts for bulk
purchases in the United States by corporations, institutions, and other
organizations. For more information, please contact the Special
Markets Department at the Perseus Books Group, 11 Cambridge
Center, Cambridge MA 02142, or call (617) 252-5298 or
(800) 255-1514, or e-mail special.markets@perseusbooks.com.

Designed by Brent Wilcox

A CIP catalog record for this book is available from the Library
of Congress
ISBN-13: 978-0-8133-4329-7 (paperback)
ISBN 0-8133-4329-1 (paperback)

07 / 10 9 8 7 6 5 4 3

Contents

Contents

Foreword

DONALDO MACEDO AND
ANA MARIA ARAÚJO FREIRE

Teachers as Cultural Workers: Letters to Those Who Dare Teach reaffirms Paulo Freire's place in history as the most significant educator in the world during the last half of this century. This insightful book represents an important answer to the capitalist "banking model" of education that has generated and continues to generate greater and greater failure. As one reads the letters to teachers contained in *Teachers as Cultural Workers*, it becomes clear why many North American liberal and neoliberal educators are looking to Paulo Freire's pedagogy as an alternative. No longer can it be argued that Freire's pedagogy is appropriate only in Third World contexts. For one thing, we are experiencing a rapid "Third-Worldization" of North America, where inner cities more and more come to resemble the shantytowns of the Third World, with high levels of poverty, violence, illiteracy, human exploitation, homelessness, and human misery. The abandonment of our inner cities and the insidious decay of their infrastructures, including their schools, make it very difficult to maintain the artificial division between the First World and the Third World. It is just as easy to find Third World misery in the First World inner cities as it is to discover First World opulence in the oligarchies in El Salvador, Guatemala, and many other Third World nations. The Third-Worldization of North American inner cities has also produced large-scale educational failures that have created minority student dropout rates that range from 50 percent in the Boston public school system to over 70 percent in the school systems of larger metropolitan areas like New York City.

Conservative educators have by and large recoiled from this landscape of educational failure in an attempt to salvage the status quo and to contain the "browning" of the United States. These conservative educators have attempted to reappropriate the educational debate and to structure the educational discourse in terms of competition and the privatization of schools. The hidden curriculum of the proposed school privatization movement consists of taking resources from poor schools that are on the verge of bankruptcy to support private or well-to-do schools. "Private school choice" is only private to the degree that it generates private profit while being supported by public funds. What is rarely discussed in the North American school debate is the fact that public schools are part and parcel of the fabric of any democratic society. In fact, conservative educators fail to recognize that a democratic society that shirks its public responsibility is a democracy in crisis. A society that equates for-profit privatization with democracy is a society with confused priorities. A democratic society that believes (falsely—one need only consider the savings and loan debacle and the Wall Street scandals, for example) that quality, productivity, honesty, and efficiency can be achieved only through for-profit privatization is a society that displays both an intellectual and ethical bankruptcy of ideas. If we accept the argument that "private" is best, we should once again consider Jack Beaty's question "Would we set up a private Pentagon to improve our public defense establishment?"[1] Would the private-is-best logic eradicate the ongoing problems in the military, problems that range from rampant sexual harassment to expenditures that are both outrageous (over $600 for a toilet seat) and wasteful (billions of dollars for airplanes that don't fly)? Most Americans would find the privatization of the Pentagon utterly absurd, claiming that a strong defense is a national priority. But we contend that instead of dismantling public education further, we should make it a national public priority. We also contend that the safeguarding of U.S. democracy rests much more on the creation of an educated, smart citizenry than on the creation of smart bombs.

In the face of market notion of school reform in the United States, many liberal and neoliberal educators have rediscovered Freire's ideas as an alternative to the conservative domestication of education that equates free-market ideology with democracy. However, part of the problem with some of these pseudocritical educators is that in the name of liberation pedagogy, they reduce Freire's leading ideas to a method. According to Stanley Aronowitz, the North American fetish for method has allowed Freire's philosophical ideas to be "assimilated to the prevailing obsession of North American education, following a tendency in all human and social sciences, with methods—of verifying knowledge and, in schools, of teaching that is, transmitting knowledge to otherwise unprepared students."[2]

This fetish for method works insidiously against the ability to adhere to Freire's own pronouncement against importing and exporting methodology. In a long conversation Paulo had with Donaldo Macedo about this issue, he said: "Donaldo, I don't want to be imported or exported. It is impossible to export pedagogical practices without reinventing them. Please tell your fellow American educators not to import me. Ask them to re-create and rewrite my ideas."

Before problematizing the reduction of Freire's leading philosophical ideas to a mechanistic method, we must comment on the "Paulo Freire Method," first, because it is still widely used today, with some adaptations, all over the world. Second, often when one speaks of Freire and literacy, one reduces Freire's thoughts on literacy to a mere set of techniques associated with the learning of reading and writing. It is necessary to clarify, especially for the sake of those who are new to Freire's thinking.

Freire's "invitation" to adult literacy learners is, initially, that they look at themselves as persons living and producing in a given society. He invites learners to come out of the apathy and the conformism—akin to being "dismissed from life"—in which they often find themselves. Freire challenges them to understand that they are themselves the makers of culture, leading them to learn the anthropological meaning of culture. They are shown that the popular classes' lower status is the result not of divine determination or fate but, rather, of the economic-political-ideological context of the society in which they live.

When men and women realize that they themselves are the makers of culture, they have accomplished, or nearly accomplished, the first step toward feeling the importance, the necessity, and the possibility of owning reading and writing. They become literate, politically speaking.

As they discuss the object to be known and the representation of reality to be decoded, the members of a "culture circle" respond to questions generated by the group coordinator, gradually deepening their readings of the world. The ensuing debate makes possible a rereading of reality from which may well result the literacy learner's engaging in political practices aiming at social transformation.

What? Why? How? To what end? For whom? Against whom? By whom? In favor of whom? In favor of what? These are questions that provoke literacy learners to focus on the substantiveness of things—that is, their reasons for being, their purpose, the way they are done, and so on.

Literacy activities require research into what Freire calls the "minimum vocabulary universe" among literacy learners. It is through work on this universe that words become chosen to integrate the literacy program. These words, about seventeen of them, called "generative words," should be phonemically rich words and necessarily ordered in increasing phonetic difficulty. They should be read within the widest possible context of the literacy learners' life and of the local language, thus becoming national as well.

Decoding the written word, which follows the decoding of a coded existential situation, implies certain steps that must be strictly followed.

Let us take the word *tijolo* 'brick', which Freire used as the first generative word in his work in Brasilia in the 1960s. This word was chosen because Brasilia was a city under construction at the time, in order to facilitate the reader's understanding.

1. The generative word *tijolo* is presented, inserted in the representation of a concrete situation: men at work at a construction site.

2. The word is simply written: *tijolo.*
3. The same word is written with its syllables separated: *ti-jo-lo.*
4. The "phonemic family" of the first syllable is presented: *ta-te-ti-to-tu.*
5. The "phonemic family" of the second syllable is presented: *ja-je-ji-jo-ju.*
6. The "phonemic family" of the third syllable is presented: *la-le-li-lo-lu.*
7. The "phonemic families" of the word being decoded are presented:

ta-te-ti-to-tu
ja-je-ji-jo-ju
la-le-li-lo-lu

This set of "phonemic families" of the generative word has been termed the "discovery form," for it allows the literacy learner to put together "pieces," that is, to come up with new phonemic combinations that will necessarily result in words of the Portuguese language.

8. Vowels are presented: a-e-i-o-u.

In sum, the moment the literacy learner is able to articulate syllables to form words, he or she is literate. The process, obviously, requires deepening, that is, a postliteracy component.

The effectiveness and validity of the "Method" lie in using the learners' reality as the starting point, in beginning with what they already know, from the pragmatic value of the things and the facts of their daily lives, their existential situations. By respecting and starting from common sense, Freire proposes overcoming it.

The "Method" follows methodological and linguistic rules but also goes beyond them, for it challenges men and women who are becoming literate to take ownership of the written code and to politicize themselves, to acquire a view of language and the world as a totality.

The "Method" rejects mere narrow-minded and mind-narrowing repetition of phrases, words, and syllables as it proposes that the learners "read the world" and "read the word," which, as Paulo Freire emphasizes, are inseparable actions. Thus he is against *"cartilhas,"* or literacy workbooks.

In short, Paulo Freire's work is more than a method for literacy education; it is a broad and deep understanding of education that has its political nature at the core of its concerns.

We would conclude these comments on the "Paulo Freire Method" by saying that the literacy education of the Brazilian people (for when Freire created the "Method" he never expected it to spread around the world) was, in the good sense of the phrase, an educational tactic designed to achieve a necessary result: the politicizing of the Brazilian people. In this sense the

"Method" is revolutionary, for it can lift those who do not yet know the written word out of their condition of submission, of immersion and passivity. The revolution as Freire envisioned it does not presuppose an inversion of the oppressed–oppressor poles; rather, it intends to reinvent, in communion, a society where exploitation and the verticalization of power do not exist, where the disenfranchised segments of society are not excluded or interdicted from reading the world.

Paulo Freire was in exile for almost sixteen years precisely because he understood education this way and because he fought to give a large number of Brazilians access to an asset traditionally denied them: the act of reading the world by reading the word.

As becomes abundantly clear, Freire's method of teaching peasants how to read was designed to be a method not as an end in itself but as part of a larger goal of politicizing the Brazilian peasants so that they could also read the world and connect the world with the word. For this reason, Freire's main ideas about the act of knowing transcend the methods for which he is known. In fact, according to Linda Bimbi: "The originality of Freire's work does not reside in the efficacy of his literacy methods, but, above all, in the originality of its content designed to develop our consciousness"[3] as part of a humanizing pedagogy. According to Freire: "A humanizing education is the path through which men and women can become conscious about their presence in the world. The way they act and think when they develop all of their capacities, taking into consideration their needs, but also the needs and aspirations of others."[4]

Freire developed students' ability to be aware of their presence in the world through the dialogic model for which he is also known. Unfortunately, many educators who embrace his notion of dialogue mechanistically reduce the epistemological relationship of dialogue to a vacuous, comfortable, feel-good zone. Reduced in this way, the dialogic model loses its clear view of the object of knowledge under study and reduces dialogue to a mere conversation about individuals' lived experiences.

With that said, we can begin to understand why some educators, in their attempt to cut the chains of oppressive educational practices, blindly advocate the dialogic model, creating, in turn, a new form of methodological rigidity laced with benevolent oppression—all done under the guise of democracy with the justification that it is for the students' own good. Many of us have witnessed pedagogical contexts in which we have been implicitly or explicitly required to speak, to talk about our experience as an act of liberation. We all have been at conferences where the speaker was chastised because he or she failed to locate himself or herself in history—because, in other words, he or she failed to give primacy to his or her experiences in addressing issues of critical democracy—regardless of the fact that the speaker had important and insightful things to say. This is tantamount to dismissing

Marx because he did not entrance us with his personal life experiences.

The dialogic method as a process of sharing experiences is often reduced to a form of group therapy that focuses on the psychology of the individual. Although some educators may claim that this process creates a pedagogical comfort zone, in our view it does little beyond making the oppressed feel good about his or her own sense of victimization. In other words, the sharing of experiences should not be understood in psychological terms only. It invariably requires a political and ideological analysis as well. That is, the sharing of experiences must always be understood within a social praxis that entails both reflection and political action. In short, it must always involve a political project with the objective of dismantling oppressive structures and mechanisms.

The overdose of experiential celebration that characterizes some strands of critical pedagogy offers a reductionist view of identity and experience within rather than outside the problematics of power, agency, and history. Educators who overindulge in the legacy and importance of their respective voices and experiences often fail to move beyond a notion or difference structured in polarizing binarisms and uncritical appeal to the discourse of experience.[5] They thus invoke a romantic pedagogical model that isolates lived experiences as a process of coming to voice. By refusing to link experiences to the politics of culture and critical democracy, these educators reduce their pedagogy to a form of middle-class narcissism. On the one hand, the dialogic method provides the participants with a group-therapy space for stating their grievances, and on the other hand, it offers the educator or facilitator a safe pedagogical zone to deal with his or her class guilt.

By refusing to deal with the issue of class privilege, the pseudocritical educator dogmatically pronounces the need to empower students, to give them voices. These educators are even betrayed by their own language. Instead of creating pedagogical structures that would enable oppressed students to empower themselves, they paternalistically proclaim: "We need to empower students." This position often leads to the creation of what we could call literacy and poverty pimps: While they are proclaiming the need to empower students, they are in fact strengthening their own privileged position.

The following example will clarify my point: A progressive teacher who had been working within a community-based literacy project betrayed her liberal discourse, her claim to want to empower the community. One of the agencies we work with solicited a colleague's help in writing a math literacy proposal for them. The colleague welcomed the opportunity and agreed. One of his goals is to develop structures that will enable community members and agencies to take the initiative and chart their own course, thus eliminating the need for our continued presence and expertise. In other words, our success in creating structures that enable community members to empower themselves rests on the degree to which our presence and expertise in the community are no longer necessary because community members have acquired their own expertise, thus preventing a type of neocolonialism.

When the progressive teacher heard about the math literacy proposal she was reticent but did not show any outward opposition. However, weeks later, when she learned that the community-based math literacy proposal written by community members competed with her own university-based proposal, which was designed to provide literacy training to community members, she reacted almost irrationally. She argued that the community agency that had written the math literacy proposal did not follow a democratic process in that it had not involved her in the development of the proposal. A democratic and participatory process, in her view, was one that necessarily included her, despite the fact that she is not a member of the particular community that the math literacy grant was designed to serve. Apparently, in her mind, one can be empowered so long as the empowerment does not encroach on the "expert's" privileged, powerful position. This is a position of power designed to paternalistically empower others.

When the obvious ideological contradictions in her behavior were pointed out, her response was quick, aggressive, and almost automatic: "I'll be very mad if they get their grant and we don't get ours." It became very clear to me that the progressive teacher's real political commitment to the community hinged on the extent to which her "expert" position remained unthreatened. That is, the literacy "expert," do-gooder, antiestablishment persona makes sure that his or her privileged position within the establishment as an antiestablishment "expert" is never absorbed by empowered community members.

It is this colonizing, paternalistic attitude that led this same progressive teacher to pronounce publicly, at a major conference, that community people don't need to go to college because, since they know so much more than do members of the university community, there is little that the university can teach them. While making such public statements, she was busily moving from the inner city to an affluent suburb, making sure that her children attend better schools.

A similar attitude emerged in a recent meeting to develop a community-university relationship grant proposal. During the meeting, a liberal white professor rightly protested the absence of community members from the committee. However, in attempting to valorize the community knowledge base, she rapidly fell into a romantic paternalism by stating that the community people knew much more than the university professors and should be invited to come to teach the professorship rather than having the professors teach the community members. This position not only discourages community members from taking advantage of the cultural capital from which these professors have benefited greatly, but it also disfigures the reality context that makes the university's cultural capital indispensable for any type of real empowerment. It also smacks of a false generosity of paternalism that Freire aggressively opposes:

> The pedagogy of the oppressed animated by authentic humanism (and not humanitarianism) generously presents itself as a pedagogy of man. Pedagogy which begins with the egoistic interests of the oppressors (an egoism cloaked in the false generosity of paternalism) and makes of the oppressed the objects of its humanitarianism, itself maintains and embodies oppression. It is an instrument of dehumanization.[6]

The paternalistic pedagogical attitude represents a middle-class narcissism that gives rise to pseudocritical educators who are part of the same instrumentalist approach to literacy that they apply to readers who meet the basic requirements of our contemporary society as proposed by conservative educators. Instrumentalist literacy also includes the highest level of literacy through disciplinary hyperspecialization. Pseudocritical educators are part of this latter instantiation of instrumentalist literacy to the extent that they reduce Freire's dialogic method to a form of specialization. In other words, the instrumentalist literacy for the poor, in the form of a competency-based skill-banking approach, and the instrumentalist literacy for the rich, the highest form, acquired through the university in the form of professional specialization, share one common feature: They both prevent the development of critical thinking that enables one to read the world critically and to understand the reasons and linkages behind the facts. The instrumentalist approach to literacy, even at the highest level of specialization (including method as a form of specialization), functions to domesticate the consciousness via a constant disarticulation between the reductionistic and narrow reading of one's field of specialization and the reading of the universe within which one's specialization is situated. This inability to link the reading of the word with the world, if not combated, will further debilitate already feeble democratic institutions and the unjust asymmetrical power relations that characterize the hypocritical nature of contemporary democracies. At the lowest level of instrumentalist literacy, a semiliterate reads the word but is unable to read the world. At the highest level of instrumental literacy achieved via specialization, the semiliterate is able to read the text of his or her specialty but is ignorant of all other bodies of knowledge that constitute the world of knowledge. This semiliterate specialist was characterized by José Ortega y Gasset as a "learned ignoramus." That is to say, "he is not learned, for he is formally ignorant of all that does not enter into his specialty; but neither is he ignorant, because he is a 'scientist' and 'knows' very well his own tiny portion of the universe."[7]

Because the "learned ignoramus" is mainly concerned with his or her own tiny portion of the world, disconnected from other bodies of knowledge, he or she is never able to relate the flux of information to gain a critical reading of the world. A critical reading of the world implies, according to Freire, "a dynamic comprehension between the least coherent sensibility of the world and a more coherent understanding of the world."[8] This explains the inability, for example, of medical specialists in the United States, who have contributed to a great technological advancement in medicine, to understand and appreciate why more than 30 million Americans do not have access to this medical technology and why we still have the highest infant mortality rate among the developed nations.

Finally, we would propose an antimethod pedagogy that refuses the rigidity of models and methodological paradigms. The antimethod pedagogy forces us to view dialogue as a form of social praxis so that the sharing of experiences is informed by reflection and political action. Dialogue as social praxis "entails that recovering the voice of the oppressed is the fundamental condition for human emancipation."[9] The antimethod pedagogy also frees us from the beaten path of certainties and specialties. It rejects the mechanization of intellectualism. In short, it calls for the illumination of Freire's leading ideas, ideas that will guide us toward the critical road of truth, toward the reappropriation of our endangered dignity, toward the reclaiming of our humanity. No one could argue more pointedly against reducing dialogue and problem posing to a mere method than Freire himself:

> Problem posing education is revolutionary futurity. Hence, it is prophetic. . . . Hence it corresponds to the historical nature of man. Hence it affirms men as beings who transcend themselves. Hence it identifies with the movement which engages men as being aware of their incompletion—an historical movement which has its point of departure, its subjects and its objective.[10]

Not only does the antimethod pedagogy adhere to Freire's view of education as revolutionary futurity, it also celebrates the eloquence of Antonio Machado's poem: "Cominante no hay camino, se trace el camino al andar [Traveler, there is no road. The road is made as one walks]." However, Freire's view of education as revolutionary futurity also requires other fundamental skills, skills that he discusses in this volume but that are seldom taught to us in our preparation as teachers:

> We must dare, in the full sense of the word, to speak of love without the fear of being called ridiculous, mawkish, or unscientific, if not antiscientific. We must dare in order to say scientifically, and not as mere blah-blah-

blah, that we study, we learn, we teach, we know with our entire body. We do all of these things with feeling, with emotion, with wishes, with fear, with doubts, with passion, and also with critical reasoning. However, we never study, learn, teach, or know with the last only. We must dare so as never to dichotomize cognition and emotion. We must dare so that we can continue to teach for a long time under conditions that we know well: low salaries, lack of respect, and the ever-present risk of becoming prey to cynicism. We must dare to learn how to dare in order to say no to the bureaucratization of the mind to which we are exposed every day. We must dare so that we can continue to do so even when it is so much more materially advantageous to stop daring.

NOTES

1. Jack Beaty, *The Boston Globe*, August 14,1992.

2. Stanley Aronowitz, "Paulo Freire's Radical Democratic Humanism," in Peter McLaren and Peter Leonard, eds., *Paulo Freire: A Critical Encounter* (London: Routledge, 1993), 8.

3. Linda Bimbi, cited in Moacir Gadotti, *Convite a Leitura de Paulo Freire* (São Paulo: Editora Scipione, 1989), 32.

4. Paulo Freire and Frei Betto, *Essa Escola Chamada Vida* (São Paulo: Atica, 1985), 14–15.

5. Henry Giroux, "The Politics of Insurgent Multiculturalism in the Era of the Los Angeles Uprising," *Journal of the Midwest Modern Language Association* 26: 1 (Spring 1993), 12–30.

6. Paulo Freire, *Pedagogy of the Oppressed* (New York: Continuum Publications, 1990), 39.

7. José Ortega y Gasset, *The Revolt of the Masses* (New York: Norton, 1932), 112.

8. Paulo Freire and Donaldo Macedo, *Literacy: Reading the Word and the World* (South Hadley, Mass.: Bergin and Garvey, 1987), 131.

9. Aronowitz, "Paulo Freire's Radical Democratic Humanism," 18.

10. Paulo Freire, cited in ibid., 11–12.

Preface:
A Pedagogy for Life

PETER MCLAREN

We live in a time that is so brutal and unforgiving that we must continually question whether we are dreaming. Even as we despairingly acknowledge the pain and desperation of so many living in the turmoil of national and international disequilibria, we still remain hapless prisoners of the illusion that we live in the best of all possible worlds. This Panglossian illusion (named after Dr. Pangloss in Voltaire's *Candide*, who responded to all unfortunate events with the comment, "All is for the best in this best of all possible worlds") has led us into an erroneous justification for perpetual war against "evil doers" and an uncritical acceptance of global capitalism. This attitude has been given ballast by our conviction that despite the farrago of wealthy sybarites and politicians whose self-interest outweighs their concern for society as a whole, we have been ordained to always be on the right side of history and that, as votaries of our Manifest Destiny, we must carry the torch of democracy to the far corners of the globe as our God-given duty, even if it means preemptive military strikes and imperialist aggression. We feel that we must trust God and our political leadership, that this is good for the cause of freedom in the long run (McLaren and Jaramillo 2005). In order for our social amnesia to remain resolutely unacknowledged, we hide behind an almost puritanical fear of any pedagogy that insists on unbolting the door to doubt, squaring our shoulders against unquestioned orthodoxy, and recognizing our entanglement in the larger conflictual arena of political and social relations and how such an entanglement is itself deeply ensconced in merging religiosity into political ends. Our merciless silence is deafening, and threatens the longevity of our social history. If we wonder how it is that here in the twenty-first century we are witnessing the steady erosion of human rights and civil liberties, the trammelling of the freedom to make history, the abandonment of the poor to the ravages of capital, as well as the devastation of our ecosystems, we only have to examine the extent of our political denial and its implication for miseducating our citizenry.

At this moment in history, Paulo Freire remains critical pedagogy's conscience-in-exile. Especially today, Freire's corpus of work threatens to explode the culture of silence that informs our everyday life as educators in the so-called world's greatest capitalist democracy. Freire sought through the pedagogical encounter and by indefatigably propagating a creed of humanism and democracy to fend off the tyranny of authoritarianism and oppression and bring about an all-embracing and diverse fellowship of global citizens profoundly endowed with a fully claimed humanity. Yet, instead of heeding a Freirean call for a multivocal public and international dialogue on our responsibility as the world's sole superpower, one that acknowledges that we Americans become defined by the way we treat others, we have permitted a fanatical cabal of truculent politicians to convince us that dialogue is weakness, an obstacle to peace, and univocal assertion is a strength.

Possibly the greatest reproach that Freire addressed to the authoritarian culture of his time was the devitalization and devaluation of human life, and the barriers to the self-development of the subject—an indictment that we must extend to all of capitalist society. It is surely striking how Freire's pedagogical commentary, by placing in our hands the responsibility to overcome the political amnesia that has become the hallmark of contemporary teaching, cannot be officially welcomed into the classrooms by the guardians of the state, for they are challenged by his language of hope and possibility. Many critics of Freire take umbrage at this storied ability to build solidarity among progressive educators at a global level. While teacher education programs have not been able to root Freire out of the philosophy of teaching, they have cannily domesticated his presence by transforming the political revolutionary with Marxist ideas into a capitalist-friendly sage who advocates a love of dialogue—separating this notion from that of a dialogue of love. Hence, there is importance in reclaiming Paulo Freire for these urgent times.

For Freire, love is preeminently and irrevocably dialogical. It is not an attachment or emotion isolated from the everyday world, including its tenebrous underside, but it emerges viscerally from an act of daring, of courage, of critical reflection. Love is not only the fire that ignites the revolutionary, but also the creative action of the artist, who covers the canvas of thought and action with a palette of sinew and spirit. Freire writes,

> We must dare in the full sense of the word, to speak of love without the fear of being called ridiculous, mawkish, or unscientific, if not antiscientific. We must dare in order to say scientifically, and not as mere blah-blah-blah, that we study, we learn, we teach, we know with our entire body. We do all of these things with feeling, with emotion, with wishes, with fear, with doubts, with passion, and also with critical reasoning (Freire 1998, 3).

On the topic of love, Freire also writes,

> [T]o the humility with which teachers perform and relate to their students another quality needs to be added: *lovingness*, without which their work would lose its meaning. And here I mean lovingness not only toward the students but also toward the very process of teach-

ing. I must confess, not meaning to cavil, that I do not believe educators can survive the negativities of their trade without some sort of "armed love," as the poet Tiago de Melo would say. Without it they could not survive all the injustice or the government's contempt, which is expressed in the shameful wages and the arbitrary treatment of teachers, not coddling mothers, who take a stand, who participate in protest activities through their union, who are punished, and who yet remain devoted to their work with students.

It is indeed necessary, however, that this love be an "armed love," the fighting love of those convinced of the right and the duty to fight, to denounce, and to announce. It is this form of love that is indispensable to the progressive educator and that we must all learn (Freire 1998, 40–41).

In addition to the quality of lovingness, Freire adds to the characteristics of the progressive teacher those of humility, courage, tolerance, decisiveness, security, the tension between patience and impatience, joy of living, and verbal parsimony, often inflecting some of these terms with nuance and poetic meaning. For instance, Freire denotes humility as the characteristic of admitting that you don't know everything; for critical citizens it represents a "human duty" to listen to those considered less competent without condescension, a practice intimately identified with the struggle for democracy and a disdain for elitism. Another example is that of tolerance. For Freire, tolerance is not understood as "acquiescing to the intolerable" or "coexistence with the intolerable" nor does it mean "coddling the oppressor" or "disguising aggression." Freire claims that tolerance "is the virtue that teaches us to live with the different. It teaches us to learn from and respect the different" (Freire 1998, 42).

Freire elaborates,

On an initial level, tolerance may almost seem to be a favor, as if being tolerant were a courteous, thoughtful way of accepting, of *tolerating*, the not-quite-desired presence of one's opposite, a civilized way of permitting a coexistence that might seem repugnant. That, however, is hypocrisy, not tolerance. Hypocrisy is a defect; it is degradation. Tolerance is a virtue. Thus if I live tolerance, I should embrace it. I must experience it as something that makes me coherent first with my historical being, inconclusive as that may sound, and second with my democratic political choice. I cannot see how one might be democratic without experiencing tolerance, coexistence with the different, as a fundamental principle (Freire 1998, 42).

Teachers as Cultural Workers is a book about according professional recognition to authentically dialogical teaching and learning. However, it is anything but the mundane connotation we have come to associate with the term "professional recognition." As Peter Mayo notes,

By professional, Freire is not referring to the excesses of the ideology of professionalism . . . based on the trait model of professionals . . . that often results in the following arrogant posture: I know what's best for you. Freire is using *profession* in the sense of people who are competent, both in terms of the subject matter taught and in terms of pedagogical disposition, and who engage in very important work that demands respect and adequate renumeration (Mayo 2004, 84).

And while *Teachers as Cultural Workers* unpacks critical pedagogy as a profession, it dialectically weaves into its discussion of teacher responsibility profound philosophical insight. Freire teaches us that truth is never about unmediated reflections on a real object—something resolutely immutable and transparent. Rather it is always dialogic, always about the self/other. In our spontaneous orientation to everyday life, we do not apply critical reasoning, and our knowledge from such unexamined experience often lacks epistemological rigor. While such knowledge should in no way be dismissed as unimportant, it is necessary to understand the importance of knowing the world systematically, by distancing ourselves from it so that we can come closer to it epistemologically and, thus, be offered what Freire calls "another kind of knowing," which he describes as "a knowing whose exactitude gives to the investigator or the thinking subject a margin of security that does not exist in the first kind of knowing, that of common sense." Freire argues that both the "innocent" knowing acquired through experience and the systematic knowledge acquired through critical reasoning "implies a debate over practice and theory that can only be understood if they are perceived and captured in their contradictory relationship." Hence, Freire warns us that neither type of knowledge is mutually exclusive and both types of knowledge must be seen in relation to each other. While we must avoid the theoretical elitism that denies the validity of common sense or experiential knowledge, we must, at the same time, avoid an anti-intellectualism that denies the importance of theoretical knowledge acquired through critical reasoning. On this note, Freire makes clear that "there is never only theory, never only practice" (Freire 1998, 93). He writes,

> Thus the sectarian political-ideological positions—positions that, instead of understanding their contradictory relationship exclude one another—are wrong. The anti-intellectualism denies validity to the theory; the theoretical elitism denies validity to the practice. The rigor with which I approach objects prohibits me from leaning toward either of these positions: neither anti-intellectualism nor elitism but practice and theory enlightening each other mutually (Freire 1998, 94).

This dialectical movement that informs theory and practice also informs our identities as social agents. Here, a dialectical tension exists between "what we inherit and what we acquire" (Freire 1998, 70). According to Freire,

> At times in this relationship, what we acquire ideologically in our social and cultural experiences of class interferes vigorously in the hereditary structures through the power of interests, of emotions, feelings, and desires, or what one usually calls "the strength of the heart." Thus we are not only one thing or another, neither solely what is innate nor solely what is acquired (Freire 1998, 70).

Freire's dialectics of the concrete is in striking contrast to the methodology of the educational postmodernists who artfully counterpose the familiar and the strange in order to deconstruct the unified subject of bourgeois humanism, resulting in a playful and often churlish hemorrhaging of certainty. Unlike the postmodernists, Freire's work retains an unshakable modernist faith in human agency consequent upon language's ineradicable sociality and dialogical embeddedness. What Freire does have in common with the postmodernists, however, is a desire to shake off the trammels of contemporary discourses that domesticate both the heart and the mind, but he is not content to remain with the postmodernists in the nocturnal world of the subconscious; rather, he is compelled to take his critical pedagogy to the streets of the real.

Freire writes,

To the extent that I become clearer about my choices and my dreams, which are substantively political and attributively pedagogical, and to the extent that I recognize that though an educator I am also a political agent, I can better understand why I fear and realize how far we still have to go to improve our democracy. I also understand that as we put into practice an education that critically provokes the learner's consciousness, we are necessarily working against myths that deform us. As we confront such myths, we also face the dominant power because those myths are nothing but the expression of this power, of its ideology (Freire 1998, 41).

Freire sees the role of teachers not as coddling parents or aunts (which helps to explain why the original Portuguese title for *Teachers as Cultural Workers* was *Professora Sim, Tia Nao*, or "teacher yes, aunt no"). Teachers do not live in a pristine world devoid of ideology, of racism, of social classes, but rather they live as social and political agents who "challenge their students, from an early to a more adult age, through games, stories, and reading so that students understand the need to create coherence between discourse and practice: a discourse about the defense of the weak, of the poor, of the homeless, and a practice that favors the haves against the have-nots; a discourse that denies the existence of social classes, their conflicts, and a political practice entirely in favor of the powerful" (Freire 1998, 15). In order to achieve this,

Freire vehemently opposes both "teacher proof" curricula and self-proclaimed specialists who hold in contempt the critical capacity of teachers to exercise a critical praxis in a coherent manner.

Ultimately, Freire's work is about reengineering the diminishing social contract by establishing a critical relationship between pedagogy and politics, highlighting the political aspects of the pedagogical and drawing attention to the implicit and explicit domain of the pedagogical inscribed in the political. While Freire extolled the virtues of socialism, and drew substantively from various Marxist traditions, he was also critical of dogmatic, doctrinaire Marxists whom he saw as intolerant and authoritarian. In fact, he ardently chastised the practice of some "mechanistic Marxists" whom he claimed believed "that because it is part of society's superstructure, education has no role to play before the society is radically transformed in its infrastructure, in its material conditions" (Freire 1998, 67). In fact, Freire argues that by refusing to take education seriously as a site of political transformation and by opposing socialism to democracy, the mechanistic Marxists have, in effect, delayed the realization of socialism for our times. Freire's Marxism was always open to a politics of possibility and hope.

As deeply religious as Freire was, nowhere does Freire say that we should act solely in the faith of our certainty or in the certainty of our faith, a faith untempered by critical analysis. Freire's afflatus derived from a mixture of religious conviction in the primacy of love and the dialectical reasoning necessary to open up the possibilities of unleashing love upon the social order. Freire criticizes those who embrace scientism as intolerant, "because they take science for the *ultimate truth*, outside of which nothing counts, believing that only science can produce certainty. Those immersed in scientism cannot be tolerant, though that fact should not discredit science" (Freire 1998, 42). Freire offers a blanket admonishment to the Left, arguing that they have often played into the hands of the reactionary Right. The Left's cardinal mistake, according to Freire, "has almost always been their absolute conviction of their certainties, which makes them sectarian, authoritarian, and *religious*. In their conviction that nothing outside of themselves made any sense, in their arrogance, in their unfriendliness toward democracy, the dominant classes had the best medium for implementing and maintaining their "dictatorship of class" (Freire 1998, 14).

Political choices and ideological paths chosen by teachers are the fundamentals of Freirean pedagogy. Freire goes so far as to say that educators "are politicians" and that "we engage in politics when we educate." And if it is the case that we must choose a political path, then let us, in Freire's words, "dream about democracy" while fighting "day and night, for a school in which we talk to and with the learners so that, hearing them, we can be heard by them as well" (Freire 1998, 68).

This is the central challenge of *Teachers as Cultural Workers* and one that requires a dauntless courage, a hopeful vision and a steadfast commitment as we struggle within and against these troubling times.

REFERENCES

Freire, P. *Teachers as Cultural Workers: Letters To Those Who Dare Teach*. Boulder, CO: Westview Press, 1998.

Mayo, P. *Liberating Praxis: Paulo Freire's Legacy for Radical Education and Politics*. Westport, CT, London: Praeger, 2004.

McLaren, P., and N. Jaramillo. "God's Cowboy Warrior: Christianity, Globalization, and the False Prophets of Imperialism." *Capitalists and Conquerors: A Critical Pedagogy Against Empire* (2005): 261–333.

Introduction

JOE L. KINCHELOE

As Peter, Shirley, and I have written, our lives have been profoundly changed by Paulo Freire. His pedagogy, his ideological orientation, his exemplary life of service, his passion for living, his radical love, his humor, and his *ad infinitum* have made us better people and challenged us to a lifetime of engagement with the world around us. For these gifts I will always be profoundly grateful to Paulo. Before writing this piece, I re-read *Teachers as Cultural Workers: Letters to Those Who Dare Teach* and, as always with a great work of intellect, I discovered that so many dimensions of the book were more important to me now than when I first read it. I found my mind drifting back to the first times I made contact with Freire's work in the early 1970s and my growing intellectual and personal closeness to him as my life progressed. For those who have or who are just now discovering Paulo, it might be interesting to know the circumstances of my own discovery of him almost three and one half decades ago.

In the early 1970s I was an undergraduate student at Emory and Henry College in the rural mountains of southwestern Virginia. As a Methodist school, Emory and Henry required six hours of religious credits. Not being innately called to southern Methodist theology, I was less than excited about the requirement and dreaded the two courses I would have to take. Looking through the catalog for the next term's offerings, I found a course entitled "The Church in the Twentieth Century." Thinking that this might not be as bad as other, more doctrinal courses, I signed up. Much to my surprise the course was interesting. Rummaging around the library looking for transgressive leftist writings about the topics of my coursework—the most valuable dimension of my undergraduate education—I was especially excited when I found a series of articles about liberation theology.

I couldn't read enough about this emerging social theology in Latin America. Theological journals were full of articles about the movement with scholars expressing both great support and vicious opposition to the liberation theologians' challenge to the status quo. I submitted a short proposal to my professor to write an essay on liberation theology as one of the important movements in Christianity in the twentieth century. I was very impressed with Dr. L., a stocky man with a black beard. He looked and acted like a scholar, and I found myself becoming very interested in learning all I could from him. I worked tirelessly on my research paper, connecting the theological dimensions of liberation theology to its social theoretical and social activist dynamics. In my early attempts at interpretation I wrote about what I considered the compelling ways that liberation theology could change the moribund mainstream Protestant religious institutions of the United States in the early 1970s. I proudly submitted the paper early. After turning it in, I hoped that such an ideologically sophisticated and savvy paper would gain me entrée to Professor L.'s scholarly mind and a chance to learn more from him.

The next week the professor entered the classroom with a few of our papers in his hand. He walked over to my desk, gave me the essay, and said he would like to meet with me after class. I was excited—I was sure that the professor would praise my work and invite me to continue my research on liberation theology in future courses. I looked at the paper—he had written nothing on it. Puzzled, but not worried, I focused my attention on class and followed Dr. L. to his office at the end of his lecture. Sitting behind his desk the professor stared at me silently for several intimidating seconds. Finally speaking, he said, "I have only one thing to say to you. Both you know and I know that you plagiarized this paper. I know that someone like you is not capable of such work. As soon as I find out where you took it from I will inform the dean of students and disciplinary action will follow. That's all I have to say."

I started to speak. I didn't know what I was going to say, but before any words came out Dr. L. raised his hand and escorted me out of his office.

I was very upset—this was the last thing I had expected. I was embarrassed; I fought back tears; I hoped I wouldn't run into anyone I knew. I replayed the "someone like you" portion of his soliloquy. In retrospect I think he was referring to my Appalachian markers: the Tennessee mountain accent, cheap clothes, the nontraditional scholarly persona. Whatever he meant, it was not a compliment.

I walked over to the library and returned to the works on liberation theology. The ideas soothed my agitated mind like an opiate. Sometime during that afternoon I found a related article on Paulo Freire—a Brazilian dissident whose political and pedagogical ideas were based on and even operationalized liberation theology. Fascinated with the politics of education, the ideological dimensions of educational practice, I was immediately drawn to Paulo. I knew that an important dimension of my relative lack of success in formal schooling had to do with the ideological frameworks I brought to the classroom in the conservative and reactive world of the American South in the 1960s and early 1970s. All of what I found exciting and emancipatory about liberation theology expressed itself in Paulo's work. Later that afternoon I found a reference to *Pedagogy of the Oppressed*. Much to my delight there was a never-checked-out copy of the book in the stacks. I began reading. The next thing I remember the lights were switched on and off as the library was closing for the night. I had been reading for hours with no sense of time, place, or the pain of my earlier encounter with Dr. L.

I returned to my dorm room with the book. I imagined Paulo working with the Brazilian peasants, teaching them to read the word and the world, developing generative themes that connected education to their everyday lives. Reading deep into the night, I noted the scholars Paulo referenced: Herbert Marcuse, Erich Fromm, Karl Marx, Georg Lukacs, Simone de Beauvoir, Frantz Fanon, Jean-Paul Sartre, Edmund Husserl, Reinhold Niebuhr, Pierre Furter, and others. In my youthful enthusiasm I promised myself that I would read all of these people. And in response to Dr. L.'s disdain of my ability to engage in the life of the mind, I vowed to know as much about the tradition Paulo learned from as I possibly could and connect it to my own egalitarian southern Appalachian ways of being. I believed I could be a transgressive scholar on my own terms. I could take my southern mountain sensibilities and with the help of liberation theology, Freirean liberatory pedagogy, the African American rhythm and blues idiom, the radical comedy of Monty Python to George Carlin and Richard Pryor, the rock spirit of Bob Dylan and John Lennon, radical revisionist historiography, and other discourses I would discover I could fashion ways of seeing and being that were my own and that contributed to larger political change.

My hope for a future where I could combine these diverse constructs in a way that would work for both personal and social transformation got me through my less-than-successful undergraduate Methodist academic experience. My sense of Freirean possibility helped me transcend the negative reactions of Dr. L. and many other professors. I desperately wanted to go to graduate school and focus my studies on these personalities and concepts. Therefore, I entered a social and cultural history master's program at the University of Tennessee in the spring of 1973. Over the next few years I continued to read Paulo and eventually got the chance to put together a Freirean reading group at the university. I was energized to be around a few people who held similar perspectives and valued the genius of Paulo Freire. We re-read *Pedagogy of the Oppressed, Education for Critical Consciousness, Cultural Action for Freedom,* and any reviews or pieces about him we could get our hands on. I was sure that Paulo would value my Appalachian background and the insights gained from living my early life as a hillbilly. I believed that he would be able to discern the connections and synergies between such a life and criticality.

It never occurred to me, however, that I would meet Paulo or become his friend—not to mention write pieces for his books. As I reflect in the middle of the first decade of the twenty-first century about how far I have come from the mountains of Tennessee and that little college in the southern Appalachian Mountains of Virginia, I am profoundly thankful for my luck and good fortune. On some level I sense that I would never have gotten to participate in the world of academia, speak to groups around the world, and write books if I hadn't encountered Paulo's work at that particular time in my life. His radical love certainly changed my life and allowed me entrée into a world I was not born to enter. Indeed, my understanding of Paulo's social vision and critical consciousness enabled me to make connections with scores of fascinating and brilliant people from all around the planet. Without Paulo's intellectual capital I would probably never have met Shirley Steinberg—our radical love and the erotic/scholarly fallout it has produced would have never existed. I would have never known that I had a zygote brother—Peter McLaren. What a loss that would have been.

Thus, it was no surprise when Donaldo Macedo arranged for Shirley and me to finally meet Paulo one autumn night in Boston that we spent four hours at Paulo's favorite Portuguese restaurant talking about radical love. One's claim of critical consciousness must affect one's romantic relationships, Paulo asserted. Such a consciousness demands a deeper, grander, and more intense type of love. To illustrate his point Paulo spoke reverently—but not sentimentally—about his relationship with his beloved wife Nita. As we listened, Shirley and I held hands under the table, knowing without speaking that the radical love

Paulo described so passionately was the basis of our relationship. We have worked to construct our lives around the concept—sometimes failing to live up to the standard, sometimes succeeding. Even with our four children, their spouses, and two grandchildren, we have labored to pass along the tradition, to embed radical love in every dimension of their lives and relationships. The personal is political, the lifeworld is inscribed by ideology, agency exists despite the ravages of structural forces, and, as Paulo put it, there is solidarity among the diverse moments of our lives.

I recall one beautiful afternoon in São Paulo at Paulo and Nita's home having the chance to talk at length with Paulo about the similarity of our childhoods in the rural mountains of Tennessee and Recife in northeastern Brazil. I have written elsewhere of how our mutual love of beans—beans and rice for Paulo and beans and cornbread for me—symbolized our shared experience of growing up in poverty-stricken areas of our two countries. After our bean bonding, Paulo opened a bottle of Beaujolais to toast our love and semiotic understanding of brown beans. It might sound bizarre to the callous, urbane sophisticate, but this was one of the most memorable moments of my life. We spoke of love, humility, writing, and the politics of football. Nita and Shirley laughed at the similarity of our ideology of sports—we labeled ourselves sports radicals. Speaking with Paulo in this and other situations always took me back to the context of my initial discovery of his work and the role it played in my bizarre Appalachian Trail to critical pedagogy.

On the occasion of the publication of the second edition of *Teachers as Cultural Workers: Letters to Those Who Dare Teach*, I imagine countless other stories about Paulo's impact on the lives of his readers. I have listened to scores of such anecdotes over the decades and trust that this volume will elicit thousands more in the coming years. Magical things happen in the transaction between Freire and reader. Such an enchanted process resides at the heart of a liberatory pedagogy, empowering those under its spell to take ownership of the formation of their selfhood, to embrace the challenge to change the world. In the reactionary political world of the twenty-first century, Paulo's impassioned spirit, critical wisdom, and radical love have never been more needed.

A Pedagogical Trap

I have just finished reading the galleys, hot off the press, before the final printing hits the bookstores, of my book *Pedagogy of Hope: A Re-Encounter with Pedagogy of the Oppressed*, which was first written in Portuguese and published by Paz e Terra in December 1992.

The title *Pedagogy of Hope* was not planned, as is sometimes the case when we write books. The title came about from discussions with friends, among them Werner Linz, the North American editor of *Pedagogy of Hope*, concerning the dynamic that takes place when the writing of a text shapes the thinking of the author. In this case, the seeds of *Pedagogy of Hope* were planted during my thinking about the major themes I elaborated in *Pedagogy of the Oppressed*. The truth is that writing is not a mere mechanical act preceded by a greater, much more important act: the act of thinking in an organized manner about a specific object, a process through which

the thinking subject begins to understand more profoundly the object of his or her thinking, a process that
will inevitably lead him or her to learn about the raison
d'être of the object of his or her thinking. This process
leads the author to know the object more intimately.
From this point on, then, the author, purely mechanically, writes about what he or she knows concerning the
object of his or her prior thinking. No! This is not exactly how these things take place. At this very moment,
even as I am writing about this process—in other words,
about the relationship between thinking, doing, writing,
reading, thought, language, and reality—I experience the
solidarity among these diverse moments that makes it
impossible to separate and dichotomize them.

This does not mean that after thinking or while I think
I should automatically write; it does mean, however, that
while I think I consciously and expressively remain aware
of the possibility of writing and that, in the same manner,
while writing I continue to think and rethink what I had
already thought before.

One of the violences perpetrated by illiteracy is the
suffocation of the consciousness and the expressiveness of
men and women who are forbidden from reading and
writing, thus limiting their capacity to write about their
reading of the world so they can rethink about their original reading of it.

Even if illiteracy does not wipe out the socially created relationships between language, thought, and real-

ity, it is a handicap that becomes an obstacle to achieving full citizenship.

Illiteracy is a handicap to the extent that in literate cultures it interdicts the illiterates by preventing them from completing the cycle in the relationship between language, thought, and reality and by closing the doors to writing, which represents an important and necessary means of understanding that relationship. We must remember that there is a dynamic movement between thought, language, and reality that, if well understood, results in a greater creative capacity. The more we experience the dynamics of such movement, the more we become critical subjects concerning the process of knowing, teaching, learning, reading, writing, and studying.

In the end, and in its more profound reading, to study involves the establishment of linkages among these relationships. It is important that I make it clear, even if I repeat myself a little, that the writing process that brings me to my desk—with my special pen, with my sheets of blank, unlined white paper (which is a precondition for me to write)—begins before I even reach my desk; it begins when I act or practice or when I fully engage in reflection concerning the object of knowledge. The writing process continues when I put down on paper, in the best way that I can, the provisional results (and they are always provisory) of my reflections. I continue to reflect while writing, thus engaging more deeply another issue that I had not taken too seriously in my earlier reflections about the object under study or about my practice.

That is why it is not possible to reduce writing to a mere mechanical act. The writing act is much more complex, and it requires more than thinking without writing.

In fact, my initial intention was to write a preface or a new introduction to *Pedagogy of the Oppressed*, in which I would rethink some of my positions by revising some of its central themes and also by addressing some of the criticism this book received and continues to receive. And it was through the process of throwing myself into this effort for months that what should have been an introduction became a new book, *Pedagogy of Hope*, almost taking the form of memories of *Pedagogy of the Oppressed*.

Similarly, even though I am still immersed in *Pedagogy of Hope*, filled with the hope that I wrote it feeling challenged by the many themes that still remain open to new reflections, I now throw myself into a new experience, just as challenging and just as fascinating: that of dealing with a theme that must be denuded to be made clearer. This does not mean, however, that as the active agent of the denuding process I have the last word regarding the truth concerning the themes under discussion.

The title *Teachers as Cultural Workers: Letters to Those Who Dare Teach* presents us with an announcement that requires a first effort if it is to be understood. In other words, we must make an effort to understand as fully as we can, an effort not simply to understand the reading of each of the constituent words of the title but to comprehend more deeply the force of reading that each individual word requires when it is inserted in a web of relationships.

The synthetic or simplified discourse, which is somewhat communicative, could be expanded as follows: My intention here is to demonstrate that the task of the teacher, who is also a learner, is both joyful and rigorous. It demands seriousness and scientific, physical, emotional, and affective preparation. It is a task that requires that those who commit themselves to teaching develop a certain love not only of others but also of the very process implied in teaching. It is impossible to teach without the courage to love, without the courage to try a thousand times before giving up. In short, it is impossible to teach without a forged, invented, and well-thought-out capacity to love. Here is how we make the link to the subtitle, *Letters to Those Who Dare Teach*. We must dare, in the full sense of the word, to speak of love without the fear of being called ridiculous, mawkish, or unscientific, if not antiscientific. We must dare in order to say scientifically, and not as mere blah-blah-blah, that we study, we learn, we teach, we know with our entire body. We do all of these things with feeling, with emotion, with wishes, with fear, with doubts, with passion, and also with critical reasoning. However, we never study, learn, teach, or know with the last only. We must dare so as never to dichotomize cognition and emotion.

We must dare so that we can continue to teach for a long time under conditions that we know well: low salaries, lack of respect, and the ever-present risk of becoming prey to cynicism. We must dare to learn how to dare in order to say no to the bureaucratization of the mind to which we are exposed every day. We must dare so that we can continue to do so even when it is so much more materially advantageous to stop daring.

None of this, however, should turn the task of teaching into a form of paternalistic coddling that leads to laissez-faire and accommodation because, in our exemplary mission as caring teachers, we cannot reconcile a nurturing posture with acts of rebellion, with protest, or with strikes by teachers, just to mention a few examples. The teaching task is above all a professional task that requires constant intellectual rigor and the stimulation of epistemological curiosity, of the capacity to love, of creativity, of scientific competence and the rejection of scientific reductionism. The teaching task also requires the capacity to fight for freedom, without which the teaching task becomes meaningless.

What seems to me to be necessary in any attempt to understand the title *Teaching as Cultural Workers: Letters to Those Who Dare Teach* is that though one should never oppose the nurturing aspect of teaching, one should never reduce teaching to merely a feel-good process, particularly to a paternalistic nurturing that takes the form of parental coddling. Teachers can have children and can therefore be parents. In the same manner, a parent can be a teacher, which means working with students. This does not, however, mean that the task of teaching transforms a teacher into his or her students' parent, nor does being a parent imply that one is automatically a teacher of his or her own children. Teaching is a profession (not the technical meaning of professionalization) that involves a specific task, a specific militancy (in the sense of advocating for students), and specific requirements for its implementation. Being a parent involves mostly the relationship of experiencing parenting. Being a teacher implies the responsibility to assume the demands of a profession, whereas parenting should not be viewed as a profession. In other words, what I am trying to make clear is the tendency in Brazil in the last three decades to reduce the role of teachers (particularly women) to a parenting role that devalues teaching—which, by its very nature, involves rigorous intellectual pursuits—by holding teachers responsible for assuaging all the ills of society, particularly the cruel and unjust presence of human misery that directly affects in multiple ways the students they teach.

The problems of teaching imply educating and, furthermore, educating involves a passion to know that should engage us in a loving search for knowledge that is—to say the least—not an easy task. It is for this reason that I stress that those wanting to teach must be able to dare, that is, to have the predisposition to fight for justice and to be lucid in defense of the need to create conditions conducive to pedagogy in schools; though this may be a joyful task, it must also be intellectually rigorous. The two should never be viewed as mutually exclusive.[1]

Refusing to identify the role of teaching with that of parenting does not in any way diminish or devalue the role of parenting. By the same token, accepting the reduction of teaching to mere parenting does not translate automatically into the valorization of teachers. It does, however, in the Brazilian context, take away certain professional responsibilities of teachers: the responsibility to be permanently engaged in a professional development that points to the realization of a political project. In the Brazilian context, this political project is undermined when teachers are reduced to a merely parental role. For example, how can parents go on strike against parenting their children? Thus the dominant ideology in Brazil, by equating teaching with mothering (which also carries low cultural currency in Brazilian society), makes it impossible for teachers to dare to go on strike to remedy the unjust conditions under which they work and through which their students are being denied their rights as citizens to the best possible education.

In my view, the refusal to identify teaching with parenting is informed, above all, by two main considerations: On the one hand, such a refusal prevents the distorted comprehension of the task of teaching, and on the other hand, it makes it easier to unveil the ideological fog that deceitfully covers the intimacy of the false identification.

The identification of teaching with parenting that has been emphasized throughout the country, particularly in private schools, is tantamount to declaring that teachers, as good parents, should never go on strike. One has never seen a thousand mothers and fathers go on strike in order to better their children's development. It is this ideology that takes away from teachers the necessary ability to protest in favor of their students by demanding better working conditions from school administrators and politicians. This ideology has enabled a great number of parents, particularly from the ruling class, to prevent teachers from exercising their duty to protest unacceptable working conditions. The same ideology also works to prevent, let us say, teachers from striking to protest the miserable working conditions in many public schools.

I still vividly remember how the former president of the association of public school teachers in the state of São Paulo, Professor Gumercindo Milhomem, responded when, some years ago, the families of students in the statewide public schools criticized teachers for striking. These families accused teachers of hurting their children by failing to meet their professional responsibilities and their duty to teach. Milhomem responded by pointing out to the families the error of their accusation: He reiterated that the striking teachers were in fact teaching their students an important lesson by giving them concrete testimony of the substantive meaning of struggle and other lessons in democracy.

9

I hold that these lessons were and are still needed in our country.

It is also important to make it clear that in talking about the ideological fog, I did not in any way mean that ruling-class parents had conspired to undermine the resistance of a sector of the working class. Nor did ruling-class parents meet secretly to obfuscate reality by creating the concept "school dropout" or by using the preposition "out" in proclaiming that "there are eight million Brazilian children out of school." The use of linguistic manipulations to hide a particular ideology does not necessarily mean that the dominant class schemed to develop discourses disguising concrete situations that in reality either push students out of school or prevent them from going to school. In reality, we do not have children who drop out of school for no reason at all, as if they just decide not to stay. What we do have are conditions in schools that either prevent them from coming to school or prevent them from staying in school. The same ideology that leads to language manipulation attempts to reduce teachers to mere coddlers.

However, even if the ideological fog has not been deliberately constructed and programmed by the dominant class, its power to obfuscate reality undeniably serves the interests of the dominant class. The dominant ideology veils reality; it makes us myopic and prevents us from seeing reality clearly.

The power of the dominant ideology is always domesticating, and when we are touched and deformed by it we become ambiguous and indecisive.[2] It is easy to understand an observation that a young teacher from the São Paulo school system made during a conversation with me: "How can we expect teachers to abandon their position as unreflective and uncritical coddlers and assume their role as teachers? [A teacher's] fear of freedom leads to a false sense of security in schools informed by a paternalistic nurturing, something that cannot exist if he or she takes on the full responsibility of a teacher."

and have one plus the other?

can't we have one plus the other?

In the ideal situation, no matter how progressive or reactionary a school administration may be, the teachers always define themselves as such. The sad reality is that they oscillate between being paternalistically well-behaved nurturers under authoritarian administrations and rebellious teachers under democratic school administrations. My hope is that by freely experimenting in open administrations teachers will maintain their commitment to freedom and their desire to create, as they must if they are going to fully assume their role as teachers, as professionals with the duty to set an example for their students and their students' families in rejecting, with dignity and energy, the arrogance and absolute will of some so-called modern administrators. But their duty to reject absolute power and authoritarianism in whatever form they take should not be done in isolation in the name of Maria, Ana, Rosália, António, or José.

This position, through which the teacher becomes a role model setting forth the values of democracy, raises three basic requirements:

[handwritten note: never let democracy change it, even if persecuted ?]

1. The project of democracy must never be transformed into or understood as a singular and individual struggle, even, as often happens, in the face of cheap persecution against this or that teacher for reasons that are purely personal.

[handwritten note: teachers are political]

2. Furthermore, teachers should always stick together as they challenge the system so that their struggle is effective.

3. Just as important as the first two requirements is that teachers exercise their right to demand and fight for permanent and ongoing teacher preparation—a preparation that is based in the experience of living the dialectical tensions between theory and practice. Teachers must think about practice in terms of developing more effective means of practice, must think about practice and begin to recognize the theory inherent in it, must evaluate practice as a means of theoretical development and not merely as an instrument to punish teachers.

[handwritten note: practice]

The evaluation of teachers' practice is necessary for a number of reasons. The first is part of the very nature of practice: All practice presents to its subjects, on the one hand, a program of action and, on the other, a continuous evaluation of the program's objectives.

However, to program and to evaluate do not represent two separate activities, one preceding the other. They represent activities that are in a permanent relationship.

The initial development of a program of study that leads to practice is sometimes changed according to insights gained from the evaluation that the practice has undergone. To evaluate almost always implies readjusting and reprogramming. For this very reason, an evaluation should never be considered the final step of a particular practice.

The second reason evaluation of practice is necessary is that the educators responsible for a program of study need to know, at each step of the way, how well they are achieving their objectives. In the end, evaluation is a process through which practice takes us to the concretization of the dream that we are implementing.

In this sense, the evaluation of practice represents an important and indispensable factor in the preparation of educators. Unfortunately, we almost always evaluate the teacher personally instead of his or her practice. We evaluate to punish and almost never to improve teachers' practice. In other words, we evaluate to punish and not to educate.

Another mistake we often make—due possibly to our loss of focus—is to evaluate students not to enhance our practice but to punish them. This is evident in our preoccupation regarding the context of our practice and our related objectives. On the other hand, this mistake manifests itself in the fact that we almost always defer our evaluation to the end of the teaching process. It seems that a good beginning for a good practice would be to evaluate the context within which the practice takes place, which means recognizing what is taking place in the context, as well as how and why it is taking place.

In this way, the critical thinking about the context, which implies its evaluation, precedes the very planning of the educational intervention that we and those we work with hope to implement in a particular context.

Even though she has criticized some aspects of such programs, Professor Madalena Freire Weffort has defended teacher-preparation groups in which teachers, directors, pedagogical coordinators, cafeteria workers, school guards, janitors, and parents participate. These groups follow the model that we developed while I was secretary of education for the city of São Paulo under the administration of Mayor Luíza Erundina. Our model differed radically from the so-called vacation courses in the traditional in-service teacher training in which the scientific preparation of those invited to teach or to give conferences did not really matter much. In general, in this context the teachers receiving training expose themselves, whether they are curious or not, to discourses by those who have been chosen as experts. This type of discourse almost always fails for a number of reasons that we know too well.

Prepackaged Teacher Education

We must scream loudly that, in addition to the activism of unions, the scientific preparation of teachers, a preparation informed by political clarity, by the capacity of teachers, by the teachers' desire to learn, and by their constant and open curiosity, represents the best political tool in the defense of their interests and their rights. These ingredients represent, in truth, real teacher empowerment. Empowerment includes, for example, teachers' refusal to blindly follow prepackaged educational materials produced by some experts in their offices to unequivocally demonstrate their authoritarianism. The development of the so-called teacher-proof materials is a continuation of experts' authoritarianism, of their total lack of faith in the possibility that teachers can know and can also create.

What is ironic in all of this is that sometimes these experts, who overload their teaching packages with detail, even explicitly promote their materials by stating that one of the main objectives of their teaching packages (though they don't call their materials "packages") is to train prospective teachers to become critical, daring, and creative. And the parody of such an expectation lies precisely in the shocking contradiction between the expressed aim and the teachers' passive behavior, enslaved by the packages themselves, domesticated by the teachers' guides, limited in their adventure to create. Their autonomy and the autonomy of their schools are restrained from producing what the prepackaged practice promises: children who enjoy freedom, who are critical and creative.

I believe that one of the tactical paths that competent and politically clear teachers must follow is to critically reject their domesticating role; in so doing, they affirm themselves professionally as teachers by demythologizing the authoritarianism of the teaching packages and their administration in the intimacy of their world, which is also the world of their students. In their classrooms, with the doors closed, it is difficult to have their world unveiled.

It is for this very reason that authoritarian administrations, even those that call themselves progressives, try through various means to instill in teachers a fear of freedom. When teachers become fearful, they begin to internalize the dominator's shadow and the authoritarian ideology of the administration. These teachers are no longer alone with their students because the force of the punitive and threatening dominant ideology comes between them.

This is the least expensive form of control, and in a way it is also the most insidious. But there is another means of control that is linked to technology. From his or her office, the school principal can control by watching or listening to what teachers do in the intimacy of their classroom.

Teachers know that the principal cannot check on twenty, fifty, two hundred teachers at the same time, but they also know that at any given moment they might be watched. Thus, inhibitions arise. In these situations, teachers become what Ana Maria Freire[3] calls "interdicted bodies." In other words, they are forbidden to be.

This type of teaching and learning must be well supported technically, and it has to be carefully guarded against any type of political teaching and learning so that

schools remain the dreams of those who intend to preserve the status quo.

Treating schools as nonneutral spaces does not mean
turning them into a political base for the party in power.
However, it is impossible to deny that the political party
running the government must have a pedagogical position that is consistent with its political options, its ideological characteristics, and its governmental practices.
Either these political preferences are recognizable, or
they are laid bare through the government's political
choices. They are explicit in the electoral campaign
phase; they are revealed in governmental plans and in
budget proposals, which are also political and not merely
technical tools.

They manifest themselves in the fundamental goals for
education, health, culture, and social programs; they are
recognizable in the politics of taxation, in the desire or
lack thereof to change the politics of public expenditures,
in the joy with which the administration prioritizes the
beautification of affluent neighborhoods while abandon-
ing the ghetto areas to decay.

In particular, how can one expect a government that
makes its elitism and authoritarianism manifest to consider in its politics the autonomy of schools?

Perhaps this contradiction could be done under the
rubric of postmodern liberalism. How can an authoritarian government allow janitors, cooks, administrators, students, and parents to really participate in schools as part

of a large community? How can one expect an authoritarian administration to govern collaboratively, to experience the good and the bad of a democratic venture?

How can one expect authoritarians to accept the challenge of learning with and from others, to tolerate difference, to accept living in the permanent tension between patience and impatience; how can one expect them not to be sure that they are right about certainties? Sectarian authoritarians live in a closed circle of their own thoughts, a circle in which they never allow doubt concerning the truth, much less its rejection. An authoritarian administration runs away from democracy like a devil from the cross.

Solidarity between a school's administration and its teachers, students, janitors, parents, and other members, a solidarity whose need we have been talking about among ourselves, would fully exist if the administration of public affairs were not truly involved with dreams and with the struggle to materialize those dreams, if the administration of a city, a state, a country were neutral. But even if all aspects of the administration of public affairs could be reduced to a purely technical task, this task could still never be neutral. And this reduction to the merely technical does not exist.

I see two central aspects in this discussion. On the one hand, we still lack a critical understanding of government, political parties, politics, and ideology. It is widely believed, for example, that administration depends entirely on the person elected to head the executive branch. Everything is expected of him or her for the first week in office. There is no understanding of government as a totality.

Recently a friend told me she had been told by her hairdresser, a regular patron of the Municipal Theater, that for years he had been convinced that there could hardly have been anyone in charge of the city's Department of Culture since its creation who was more competent and critically committed to it than was Marilena Chaui. "I didn't vote for Suplicy, however," said my friend's hairdresser, "because Erundina, just as PT[4] as she is, did not undertake any major projects." To this man, a lover of the arts, dance, music, and culture, none of what had been achieved by the Department of Culture had anything to do with Erundina; and furthermore, none of it could be listed under *major projects*.

"When we took over the city's Department of Education," recently declared the then secretary Mário Cortela (I was witness to this fact), "63 percent of its schools had deteriorated, some were actually condemned. We now leave the department with 67 percent of its schools in excellent condition."

Only overpasses, tunnels, and landscaped squares in the fortunate sections of the city would qualify as major projects.

The second aspect I would like to focus on here is the responsibility of citizenship. We will only come to terms

19

with this problem through a critical awareness of our social and political responsibility as a civil society, a responsibility not to take over the state's role, letting it sleep undisturbed, but to learn to mobilize and organize so that we can better supervise the state as it fulfills or fails to fulfill its constitutional duty. Only this way will we be able to move toward a broad dialogue, at the center of society, bringing together its legitimate representatives and political parties, both conservative and progressive, in order to set limits compatible with the different interests of society's various segments, that is, limits to which these different political-ideological forces could accommodate to bring about continuity in public administration.

It seems lamentable to me that material projects and social programs should be abandoned primarily or even exclusively because the new administrators have personal grudges against their predecessors and thus paralyze something of social significance.

On the other hand, I cannot see why, or how, an administration that takes office on the basis of progressive discourse and proposals should maintain, in the name of administrative continuity, programs that are undeniably elitist and authoritarian.

Neoliberal discourse sometimes criticizes progressive candidates and parties, accusing them of being obsolete because they are ideological; they say that the people no longer accept such discourse, that they now accept only technical and competent discourses. But there is no technical and competent discourse that is not naturally ideological as well.

As I see it, what the people refuse more and more, above all when it comes to progressive parties, is the parties' antihistorical insistence on behaving like Stalinists. Some progressive parties lose their sense of history and behave in a way reminiscent of traditional movements from the beginning of the century, threatening and suspending activists whose behavior does not please them. The leadership of such groups does not realize that they could not survive even if they were to keep themselves current, let alone if they stay traditionally arbitrary. History requires them to become postmodernly progressive. That is what the people expect; that is what voters, sensitive to and synchronized with history, dream of.

I believe that what the people reject is sectarian verbiage and aged slogans; it has not always been easy for us to realize that one cannot, in critical terms, expect a popular government from an authoritarian and elitist candidate or party. In seeking a greater understanding of what constitutes good or bad public spending policy, which is associated with the issue of what is or is not a major project, we are led into distortions. I do not believe we can overcome the causes of such distortions only by working through factual obstacles, by being more critically aware of objective data about reality. We have to work through ideological obstacles; if we do not, we cannot pave the way for a lucid realization, for example, that between me and the candidate I vote for there is much more than an affective relationship or one of gratitude. If I am thankful to a reactionary person, I can and should express my gratitude to him or her. But my gratitude cannot become involved in public interest. If my utopia, my dream, for which I fight side by side with so many others, is the antagonistic opposite of the reactionary candidate's dream, I cannot vote for him or her. My gratitude must not lead me to working against my dream, which is not exclusively mine. I do not have the right to expose that dream to *pay* a *debt* that is mine alone.

Voting for candidate A or B is not a matter of helping A or B become elected but, rather, of delegating to someone at a certain level of political power the possibility of fighting for a possible dream. Under no circumstances, then, can I or should I vote for someone who, if elected, will fight against my dream.

It is unbelievable that we continue to vote for progressive candidates to the executive branch but for reactionary ones to the legislature simply because they may have used their position to help us at some point.

Let us return for a moment to the understanding of what is considered a major project. This understanding is strongly marked by the dominant ideology. Just as only those who have power define or determine who does not, they also define what is in good taste, what is ethical, what is beautiful, and what is good. The popular classes, subordinate as they are, obviously internalize many of the dom-

inant ideology's value criteria, just as they do the dominant ideology. However, we must recognize that this is a
dialectic process, not a mechanical one. Thus the popular
classes at times—especially when they find themselves experimenting with the struggle for their rights and interests—resist the dominant classes' attempt to subjugate
them. Sometimes they remake the dominant ideology
with their own elements. In any case, however, to many
members of the popular classes major projects are those
that are also deemed so by the dominant classes. Avenues,
gardens, the beautification of what is already beautiful in
the city, tunnels, and overpasses are projects that might
undeniably be somewhat in the interest of the popular
classes, given that the city is a whole, a totality. They do
not, however, meet the primary needs of the popular
classes, whereas they do meet those of the well-off classes.

I do not want to even suggest that a progressive, democratic, radical, but nonsectarian administration would stop
responding to the challenges with which it struggles in
the richer areas of the city solely because they *are* the
problems of the rich. Rigorously speaking, the problems
of the city are the city's problems: They do affect both
the rich and the poor, although certainly in different
ways. What is not acceptable is that a progressive administration should not feel compelled by a duty they may
not decline to prioritize public spending as a function of
the real, glaring, and often dramatic needs of exploited
populations.

major project do's + don'ts for progressives

A serious, democratic, and progressive administration must not hesitate between, on the one hand, beautifying the already beautiful and allowing the rich to avoid paying taxes and, on the other, paving kilometers of streets in the dispossessed and ignored areas of the city, taking care of sanitation, building schools (with which we could reverse the quantitative deficit in our education, which is not observed in the *fortunate* sections of the country), providing enough and ever-better health care, multiplying the number of day care centers, or caring for the people's cultural expression.

I have tried to make clear my thesis that since the Right continues to exist, progressive or left political parties must not fall for the argument that ideologies are gone, and that from this starting point they must move to understanding the political struggle as a colorless, odorless dispute. It is a dispute in which only technical competence and competence in better communicating the government's aims and objectives really matter.

It is interesting to observe that the victorious candidate in a past São Paulo mayoral race insisted that he only proposed "issues of an *administrative* nature and not of a *political* or *ideological* one." And he did not do so without revealing his great effort in convincing himself that *administrative issues*, pure and chaste, untouched by the *ideological* and the *political*, are indeed neutral.

There has never been such a savvy administrator, one who could touch the world, interfere in it, with the jus-

tice of his or her technical knowledge, one so great and so
pure as to be seductive. Such a person would have the
power to abolish social classes; to ignore the fact that existential differences between the rich and the poor necessarily generate, in different people, different ways of
being, different likes and dreams, different cultures, and
different ways of thinking, of acting, of valuing, of speaking; and to ignore the fact that all this has to do with political choices, with ideological paths.

The more the Left allows itself to dance to this tune,
the less pedagogically it is acting and the less it contributes to the development of critical citizenship. Thus
my insistence in repeating that the progressives make a
mistake in not producing campaigns with ideological
content. Such campaigns should be made better and better, making it clear to the popular classes that class differences (which they at the very least have a sensory
knowledge of; it comes to them through their skins, their
bodies, their souls) cannot be denied and that class differences have everything to do with political projects,
with the aims of the government, and with its composition. They must understand that electoral discourse is
one thing and that postelection reality is another. Fer-
nando Affonso Collor de Mello called himself the candidate of the shirtless, and yet never have the shirtless
among us been more naked and tragically lost than during the period of absurdity and lack of decorum that was
his government.

The mistake of the Left has almost always been their absolute conviction of their certainties, which makes them sectarian, authoritarian, and *religious*. In their conviction that nothing outside of themselves made any sense, in their arrogance, in their unfriendliness toward democracy, the dominant classes had the best medium for implementing and maintaining their "dictatorship of class."

The mistake today, or rather the risk, is that, stunned by all that has happened since the changes in the former Soviet Union, the Left may either reactivate the fear of freedom, the aversion to democracy, or apathetically succumb to the myth of capitalist excellence, thus wrongly accepting that political campaigns are not ideological. There is yet another mistake or risk, that of believing in reactionary postmodernity, according to which the death of ideology has led to the disappearance of social classes, dreams, and utopias as well, making public administration purely a technical matter, detached from politics and ideology.

These mistakes are the only explanation for the fact that up until recently leftist activists would accept posts in governments that were contrary to their erstwhile convictions. If there are no longer social classes, if everything is more or less the same thing, if the world has gone opaque, the technical instruments with which such a world operates cannot be any less murky.

That the dominant classes would disseminate the ideology of ideological death, whether believing or disbelieving it, seems like behavior typical of them.

That a person who was progressive yesterday should become reactionary today seems possible, if regrettable. What I cannot accept is for this leap from one extreme to the other to be spoken of as if, because there are no more poles, no left, no right, one had simply walked or moved on the same plane, as if the move was technical, *odorless, colorless, tasteless*. No, not that!

Teaching Is Not Coddling

Why do I allow myself to detour from the basic issue of the role of teachers as teachers and not as coddling parents? It is exactly because this detour is purely fictitious.

The attempt to reduce teachers to the status of coddling parents represents an "innocent" ideological trap in that, under the illusion of softening teachers' lives, what is in fact being attempted is to soften the teachers' capacity to struggle or to keep them occupied in the implementation of their day-to-day tasks. For example, teachers' capacity to struggle involves their capacity to challenge their students, from an early to a more adult age, through games, stories, and reading so that students understand the need to create coherence between discourse and practice: a discourse about the defense of the weak, of the poor, of the homeless, and a practice that favors the haves against the have-nots; a discourse that denies the existence of social classes, their conflicts, and a political practice entirely in favor of the powerful.

It does not seem right to me to defend or to simply accept as normal the profound difference that sometimes exists between a candidate's preelection and postelection positions. It does not seem ethical to me to live this way or to defend this contradiction as acceptable behavior. It is not with these kinds of practices that we foster a vigilant citizenry, which is indispensable to the development of democracy.

Finally, the thesis that teachers should be teachers and not coddling parents points to the fact that we all have the privilege and the duty to fight for the right to be ourselves, to opt, to decide, and to unveil truths.

Thus a teacher is a teacher whereas a parent (coddling or not) remains a parent. It is possible to be a parent without loving one's children, without even liking being a parent, but it is not possible to be a teacher without loving one's students, even realizing that love alone is not enough. It is not possible to be a teacher without loving teaching. But it is easier, as a teacher, to say that one does not like to teach than, as a parent, to say that one does not like that role. Reducing teachers to the role of parents implies playing with parents' inherent fear of rejecting their roles as such.

It is also possible to be a teacher without struggling for the rights that would enable one to carry out one's duty as a teacher. But the reader of this book retains the right, in being a teacher or in pretending to be, to want to view his or her teaching role as a form of parental coddling.

28

NOTES

1. See the work of George Snyders, *La Joie à l'école* (Paris: PUF, 1986).

2. Anoréa Pellegrini Marques.

3. Ana Maria Freire, *Analfabetismo no Brasil: Da Ideologia da interdição do corpo a ideologia nacionalista ou de como deixar sem ler e escrever desde as catarinas (paraguaçu), filipas, madalenas, anas, genebras, apolonios e gracias até os severinos* (São Paulo: Cortez Editora, 1995).

4. PT stands for Partido Trabalhista, the Workers' Party.

Reading the World/
Reading the Word

No topic could be a better subject for this first letter to those who dare teach than the critical significance of teaching and the equally critical significance of learning. There is no *teaching* without *learning*, and by that I mean more than that the act of teaching demands the existence of those who teach and those who learn. What I mean is that teaching and learning take place in such a way that those who teach learn, on the one hand, because they recognize previously learned knowledge and, on the other, because by observing how the novice student's curiosity works to apprehend what is taught (without which one cannot learn), they help themselves to uncover uncertainties, rights, and wrongs.

The learning of those who teach does not necessarily take place through their apprentices' rectification of their mistakes. Their learning in their teaching is observed to

the extent that, humble and open, teachers find themselves continually ready to rethink what has been
thought and to revise their positions. Their learning lies
in their seeking to become involved in their students' curiosity and in the paths and streams it takes them
through. Some of the paths and streams that students' at
times almost virgin curiosity runs through are pregnant
with suggestions and questions never before noticed by
teachers. But now, as they teach, not as *bureaucrats of the
mind* but reconstituting the steps of their curiosity—the
reason their conscious bodies, sensitive and touched,
open up to the students' *guesses*, their innocence, and
their discrimination—teachers who perform as such have
a rich moment of learning in their teaching. Teachers first
learn how to teach, but they learn how to teach as they
teach something that is relearned as it is being taught.

The fact, however, that teachers learn how to teach a
particular content must not in any way mean that they
should venture into teaching without the necessary competence to do it. It does not give persons a license to
teach what they do not know. Teachers' political, ethical,
and professional responsibility puts them under an obligation to prepare and enable themselves before engaging
in their teaching practice. Teaching requires constant
preparation and development on the part of teachers, as is
made clearer and clearer by their teaching experience, if
well lived and apprehended. Such development is based
on a critical analysis of their practice.

Let us begin from the learning, uncovering experience of those who are preparing for the teaching task, which necessarily involves *studying*. Obviously, my intention here is not to prescribe rules that must be strictly followed; that would be in shocking contradiction to everything I have talked about so far. On the contrary, what I am concerned with here, in line with the spirit of this book, is challenging its readers around certain points and aspects, demonstrating that there is always something different to be done in our educational day-to-day, whether we are involved in it as learners, and thus as teachers, or as teachers, and thus as learners as well.

I would not like to even give the impression that I am seeking to absolutely clarify the issues of *studying*, of *reading*, of *observing*, of *recognizing* the relationship between objects in order to get to know them. I will be trying to clarify some points that deserve our attention for a more critical understanding of these processes.

Let us begin with *studying*, which though involving *teaching* on the part of the teacher also involves a previous and concomitant learning on the part of the teacher and a learning either by students who are preparing to teach tomorrow or re-creating their knowledge to better teach today or by those who, children still, find themselves in the initial stages of their schooling.

An individual's preparation for learning, studying, is before anything else a critical, creative, re-creating activity. It does not matter whether one engages in it through reading a text that deals with and discusses a certain content proposed by a *school* or whether one starts from critical reflection on a certain social or natural occurrence that then leads to the reading of texts suggested by one's own curiosity or intellectual experience or suggested by others.

Thus, from a critical perspective, one that does not dichotomize between commonsense knowledge and the other more systematic, more precise knowledge but, rather, seeks a synthesis of opposites, the act of *studying* always implies that of reading, even if it is not reduced to it. Reading of the word enables us to read a previous reading of the world. But reading is not purely entertainment, nor is it a mechanical exercise in memorization of certain parts of a text.

If I am really studying, seriously reading, I cannot go past a page if I cannot grasp its significance relatively clearly. My solution does not lie in memorizing portions of paragraphs by mechanically reading—two, three, four times—portions of the text, closing my eyes and trying to repeat them as if the simple machinelike memorization could give me the knowledge I need.

Reading is an intellectual, difficult, demanding operation, but a gratifying one. Nobody studies authentically who does not take the critical position of being the subject of curiosity, of the reading, of the process of discovery. Reading is searching for, seeking to create an understanding of what is read; thus, among other fundamental points, the correct teaching of reading and writing is of great importance. It is not just that teaching reading is engaging; it is a creative experience around *comprehension*, comprehension and communication. And the experience of comprehension will be all the deeper if we can bring together, rather than dichotomizing, the concepts emerging from the school experience and those resulting from the day-to-day world. One critical exercise always required in reading, and necessarily also in writing, is that of easily moving from *sensory experience*, which characterizes the day-to-day, to *generalization*, which operates through school language, and then on to the tangible and concrete. One of the ways we can accomplish this exercise is through the practice that I have been referring to as "reading of a previous reading of the world," and here, "reading of the world" should be understood as the "reading" that precedes the reading of the word and that, equally concerned with the comprehension of objects, takes place in the domain of day-to-day life. The reading of the word, also a function of a search for text comprehension and thus of the objects contained therein, directs us now to a previous reading of the world. I must make it clear that this reading of the world, which is based on sensory experience, is not enough. But on the other hand, it must not be dismissed as inferior to the reading of the abstract world of concepts that proceeds from generalization to the tangible.

A literacy student from the northeast was discussing, in her culture circle, a codification[1] representing a man who created a clay vase with his own hands. The discussion involved the "reading" of a series of codifications, which in fact are representations of concrete reality, which is culture.

The concept of culture had already been apprehended by the group through the effort of *comprehension*, which characterizes the reading of the world or the *word*. The woman's memories of her previous experience and her sensory understanding of the process by which the man worked the clay to create the vase told her that the making of the vase was the sort of work with which he made a living. Just as the vase was only an object, it was the product of his work, which, once sold, made his and his family's lives viable.

Now, going beyond the sensory experience, the woman took a fundamental step: She reached the ability to *generalize*, which characterizes "school experience." Creating a vase through transformative work over clay was no longer only a means of survival but was also a means of creating *culture*, of creating *art*. For this reason, by revisiting her previous reading of the world, of the day-to-day activities in the world, that northeastern literacy student, proud and secure, said, "I create culture. I do this."

I have also had the opportunity to witness a similar experience from the point of view of the intelligence of people's behavior. I have referred to this fact before in my writing, but there is no harm in bringing it up again.

I found myself on the island of São Tomé, in the Guinea Gulf off the western coast of Africa. I was with local educators, taking part in the first development program for literacy teachers.

The national commission had picked the small village of Porto Mont, a fishing community, as the center of all program activities. I suggested to the local educators that the development program not follow certain traditional methods that tend to separate theory from practice and that we not engage in any sort of work or activity that essentially dichotomized theory and practice either by underestimating *theory*, denying it any importance, by exclusively emphasizing *practice* as the only thing to really count, or by undermining practice by focusing only on theory. On the contrary, my intention was to have, from the very beginning, direct experimentation with the contradictions between theory and practice, which will be the object of analysis in one of my letters.

I refused, for this very reason, a schedule that reserved the initial moments for so-called theoretical presentations on fundamental content for the development of the future educators. In essence, that meant moments reserved for the speeches of the people deemed better able to speak before others.

My conviction lay elsewhere. I was thinking of a sequence of activities in which, in just one morning, we could discuss some key concepts—codification and decodification, for example—as if it were a time for *presentation* but without thinking even for a second that presentations were sufficient for the mastery of certain concepts. What was needed was a critical discussion of the practice in which the educators were about to engage.

Thus, with that basic idea accepted and put into practice, the future educators were asked to coordinate a discussion about codifications in a culture circle with twenty-five participants, who were aware that the activity addressed the professional development of educators. Prior to that, a discussion had been held about the political nature of their task, the task of helping us in a professional development effort, and they knew that they were going to be working with young people in a process of professional development. They knew that neither the teachers they were to work with nor they themselves had ever done anything like what they were going to do. The only difference that marked them was that the participants could only read from the world, while the young teachers in training read the word as well. They had never, however, discussed any codifications or taught literacy before.

Each afternoon in the program, four trainees took charge of the two-hour work sessions with the twenty-five participants. Those responsible for the program watched silently, taking notes. The theory behind the trainees' actions was revealed the following day during the four-hour evaluation and development seminars, when the mistakes, the errors, and the good points in their performance were discussed in the presence of the entire group.

The glitches and mistakes that had
and analyzed were hardly ever repeate
soaked in well-carried-out practice.

During one of these afternoon sessio
about a codification depicting Porto N
houses lined up along the beach, facin
fisherman who walked away from his boat holding a fish—
two of the participants stood up, as if they had planned it,
walked to the window of the school where we were, looked
at Porto Mont in the distance, and faced the codification
that depicted the village once again and said, "Yeah, this is
what Porto Mont is like, and we didn't even know it!"

Up until that point, their "reading" of that locale, of
their private world, a reading made extremely close to the
"text," which was the context of the village, had pre-
vented them from *seeing* Porto Mont as it was. A certain
dullness had veiled Porto Mont. The experiment they
were conducting, of "taking some distance" from the object, the Porto Mont *codification*, allowed them to make a
new reading, one more truthful to the text, to the context
of Porto Mont. The taking of distance that the reading of
the codification afforded them brought them closer to
Porto Mont as a text being read. This new reading re-
created their previous reading; that is why they said: "This
is what Porto Mont is like, and we didn't even know it!"
Immersed in the reality of their small world, they were
unable to *see* it. By taking some distance, they *emerged*
and were thus able to see it as they never had before.

study is to uncover; it is to gain a more exact *comprehension* of an object; it is to realize its relationships to other objects. This implies a requirement for risk taking and venturing on the part of a student, the subject of learning, for without that they do not create or re-create.

For this reason also, as I have said so many times, *teaching* cannot be a process of transference of knowledge from the one teaching to the learner. This is the mechanical transference from which results machinelike memorization, which I have already criticized. Critical study correlates with teaching that is equally critical, which necessarily demands a critical way of comprehending and of realizing the reading of the word and that of the world, the reading of text and of context.

This critical way of comprehending and realizing the reading of the word and of the world lies, on the one hand, in not dismissing simpler language, "unguarded," innocent language. It lies in not devaluing such language because it is based on concepts developed in day-to-day experience, in the world of sensory experience. On the other hand, it also lies in moving away from the concept of "difficult language," impossible language, as development occurs around abstract concepts. This critical way of comprehending and realizing the reading of text and context does not exclude either variety of language, of syntax. It does recognize, however, that writers using scientific, academic language cannot become simplistic even though they must attempt to become more accessible, clearer, simpler, less closed, and less difficult.

No one who reads has the right to abandon the reading of a text because it is difficult, because he or she does not understand the meaning, for example, of a word such as *epistemology*.

Just as bricklayers require a collection of tools and instruments, without which they cannot build up a wall, student-readers also require fundamental instruments, without which they cannot read or write effectively. They require dictionaries,[2] including etymological dictionaries, dictionaries focusing on verbs and those looking at nouns and adjectives, philosophical dictionaries, thesauruses, and encyclopedias. They need comparative readings of texts, readings by different authors who deal with the same topics but with varying degrees of language complexity.

Using these tools is not, as many may think, a waste of time. The time one spends when one reads or writes, or writes and reads, on the use of dictionaries or encyclopedias, on the reading of chapters or fragments of texts that may help a more critical analysis of a topic, is a fundamental component of one's pleasurable task of reading or writing.

When we read, we do not have the right to expect, let alone demand, that writers will perform their task, that of writing, and also ours, that of comprehending the text, by explaining every step of the way, through footnotes, what they meant by this or that statement. Their duty as writers is to simply and *lightly* write, making it easier for the reader to attain understanding but without doing the reader's job.

A reader does not suddenly comprehend what is being read or studied, in a snap, miraculously. Comprehension needs to be worked, forged, by those who read and study; as subjects of the action, they must seek to employ appropriate instruments in order to carry out the task. For this very reason, *reading* and *studying* form a challenging task, one requiring patience and perseverance. It is not a task for those who, excessively hurried or lacking humbleness, transfer their weaknesses to the author, whom they then blame for being impossible to study.

It is important to make clear, also, that there is necessarily a relationship between the level of content in a book and the reader's actual level of development. These levels depend on the intellectual experience of both reader and author. The comprehension of what is read is tied to this relationship. When those levels are too far apart, when one has nothing to do with the other, all efforts toward *comprehension* are fruitless. In such cases, there is no consonance between the author's view of the necessary treatment of the topic and the reader's ability to apprehend the language required for that treatment of the topic. That is why studying is a preparation for knowing; it is a patient and impatient exercise on the part of someone whose intent is not to know it all at once but to struggle to meet the *timing* of knowledge.

The issue of the necessary use of the instruments indispensable to the task of reading and the work of writing raises a concern with the purchasing power of students and teachers, in light of the high costs of basic dictionaries, philosophical dictionaries, and so on. Being able to have access to such resources is a material right of students and teachers alike; this right corresponds to schools' duty to make these materials available by creating and furnishing libraries that are open on realistic schedules. Demanding this access is a right and duty of students and teachers alike.

I would now like to return to something I referred to previously: the relationship between reading and writing, which should be understood as processes that cannot be separated. They should be understood as processes that must be organized in such a way as to create the perception that they are needed for something, a perception, as Lev S. Vygotsky[3] emphasized, of being something that children need and that we too need.

Initially, oral expression precedes writing, but writing has encompassed oral expression ever since the moment humans became able to express themselves through symbols that said something about their dreams, their fears, their social experience, their hopes, and their practices.

When we learn how to *read*, we do it upon the writing of someone who previously learned how to read and write. As we learn how to read, we are preparing to immediately write the talk we socially construct.

In the literate cultures, without reading and writing it is impossible to study, to seek to know, to learn the subjectivity of objects, to critically recognize an object's reason for being.

One of the mistakes we often make is to dichotomize reading and writing and, even from children's earliest steps in the practice of reading and writing, to conceive of these processes as detached from the general process of knowing. This dichotomy between reading and writing follows us forever, as students and as teachers. "I have a tremendously hard time writing my papers. I cannot *write*" is the comment I hear most frequently in the graduate programs I have been involved with. Deep down, this fact reveals the sad fact of how far we are from a critical understanding of what it means to teach and to learn.

It is important that we take critical ownership of the formation of our selves, which socially and gradually, over time, become active and conscious, speaking, reading, and writing, and which are both inherently and socially constructed. In other words, we must not only realize what we are, but we must also fully embrace ourselves as these beings "programmed for learning," as François Jacob[4] put it. Then we must learn how to learn; in other words, we must, among other things, recognize that oral and written language, their use, are equally important objectively.

Those we study, and those we teach and thus study as well, require that we not only read texts but write notes, write book reports, and compose small texts about the things we read. We must read the works of good writers; of good novelists, poets, scientists, and philosophers; of those who do not fear working their language in search of beauty, simplicity, and clarity.[5]

If our schools, from the earliest grades, were to devote themselves to the work of nurturing in students a taste for reading and writing and were to maintain that nurturing throughout their school lives, there would possibly be fewer graduate students who spoke of their inability to write or their insecurity about writing.

If studying were not almost always a *burden* to us, if reading were not a bitter obligation, if, on the contrary, studying and reading were sources of pleasure and happiness as well as sources of the knowledge we need to better move about the world, we would have indexes that were more indicative of the quality of our education.

This is an effort that should be initiated in grammar school, should be intensified during the stages of literacy development, and should continue without ever stopping.

It is undeniably important to read the works of Jean Piaget, of Lev S. Vygotsky, of Emilia Ferreiro, of Madalena F. Weffort, among others, as well as to read the work of specialists who deal, strictly speaking, not with literacy but with the reading process, such as Marisa Lajolo and Ezequiel T. da Silva.

If we think about the intimate relationship between reading, writing, and thinking and about our need to intensely experience this relationship, we might accept the suggestion that at least three times a week we should devote ourselves to the task of writing something. That writing could be notes about something read, a commentary about some event reported in the media, a letter to an unknown person—it doesn't matter what. It is also a good idea to date and keep these writings and, a few months later, critically analyze them.

Nobody can write who never writes, just as one cannot swim who never swims.

Though I underscore here that the use of written language, and thus of reading, is tied to a society's material development, I would like to emphasize that my position is not an *idealistic* one.

Just as I refuse any *mechanistic* interpretation of history, I refuse any *idealistic* one as well. The former reduces conscience to a mere copy of society's material structures; the latter subjects everything to an all-powerful conscience. My position is a different one: I understand that these relationships between conscience and the world are dialectic.[6]

What is not appropriate is for us to wait for material transformations before we begin to face up to the problem of reading and writing correctly.

A critical reading of the texts and of the world has to do with the changes in progress within them.

NOTES

1. About codification, reading of the reading world, of the sense word, exact common knowledge, learning, and teaching, see Paulo

Freire, *Education as the Praxis of Freedom* (Rio de Janeiro: Paz e Terra), *Education and Change* (Rio de Janeiro: Paz e Terra), *Cultural Action for Freedom* (Rio de Janeiro: Paz e Terra), *Pedagogy of the Oppressed* (Rio de Janeiro: Paz e Terra, 1970), *Pedagogy of Hope: A Return to the Pedagogy of the Oppressed* (Rio de Janeiro: Paz e Terra, 1992), and *The Importance of the Reading Act* (São Paulo: Cortez, 1992); Paulo Freire and Sergio Guimaraes, *About Education* (Rio de Janeiro: Paz e Terra, 1987); Paulo Freire and Ira Shor, *Fear and Daring: The Educator's Day-to-Day* (Rio de Janeiro: Paz e Terra); Paulo Freire and Donaldo Macedo, *Literacy, Reading of the World, and Reading of the Word* (Westport, Conn.: Bergin and Garvey, 1987); Paulo Freire and Marcio Campos, "Reading of the World—Reading of the Word," *Courrier de L'UNESCO* (February 1991).

2. See Freire, *Pedagogy of Hope.*

3. Luis C. Moll, ed., *Vygotsky and Education. Instructional Implications and Applications of Sociohistorical Psychology,* 1st paperback ed. (Cambridge and New York: Cambridge University Press, 1992).

4. François Jacob, "Nous sommes programmé mais pour apprendre," *Courrier de L'UNESCO* (February 1991).

5. See Freire, *Pedagogy of Hope.*

6. To this end see Freire, *Pedagogy of Hope.*

Don't Let the Fear of What Is Difficult Paralyze You

I believe the best way to begin is by considering the whole issue of difficulty, of what it is that is difficult and that triggers fear.

It is said that something is difficult when facing it or dealing with it proves painstaking; in other words, when it presents an obstacle on some level. "Fear," as defined by the *Aurélio Dictionary*, is a "feeling of unrest before the notion of real or imaginary danger." We fear weathering a storm. We fear loneliness. We fear not being able to overcome the difficulties involved in understanding a text.

There is always a relationship between fear and difficulty. But it is obvious that in this relationship the subject also figures, a subject who is fearful of what is difficult, who fears the storm, who fears loneliness, or who fears not being able to overcome the difficulty in understanding the text or not being able to produce some intelligence of it.

In this relationship between the *subject* who fears and the situation or object of that *fear*, there is yet another component, which is the fearful subject's feeling of *insecurity* in facing the obstacle. This insecurity may be based on the subject's lack of physical strength, lack of emotional balance, or lack of scientific competence, real or imaginary.

The issue here is not denying fear when the danger that generates it is fictitious. The fear itself is concrete. The issue is not allowing that fear to paralyze us, not allowing that fear to persuade us to quit, to face a challenging situation without an effort, without a fight.

When faced with fear of any kind, one must first objectively ascertain whether there are real reasons for that fear. Second, if those reasons do exist, one must match them against the available possibilities for overcoming them successfully. Third, if an obstacle cannot be overcome right away, one must determine what steps to take toward becoming better capable of overcoming it tomorrow.

I wish to emphasize that *difficulty* is always in direct relation to an individual's capacity to respond to it, in light of his or her own evaluation of the ability to respond. One may experience more or less fear or unfounded fear; one may even, when realizing that a challenge surpasses the limits of fear, drown in *panic*. Panic is the state of mind that paralyzes an individual faced with a challenge that he or she easily identifies as absolutely beyond any possible attempt to respond. I can be in fear of loneliness, but I experience *panic* in a city struck by an earthquake.

At this point I would like to reflect specifically on one's fear of not being able to understand a text whose comprehension is necessary to the discovery process that is part of education. I would like to focus on that paralyzing fear that defeats us even before we make any attempt to understand the text.

If one takes on a text whose comprehension will require some work, one needs to know

- whether one's ability to respond is at the level of the challenge posed, that is, the challenge of understanding the text.
- whether one's ability to respond is less than needed to meet the challenge.
- whether one's ability to respond is more than needed to meet the challenge.

If one's ability to respond is *less* than needed to meet a given challenge, one must not allow oneself to be immobilized by the *fear* of not understanding or, by defining the task as impossible to realize, to simply abandon it. If my ability to respond to a text is less than needed to comprehend the text, I must seek the help of someone, not just the teacher who assigned the reading, in overcoming at least some of the limitations that make the task more difficult. Sometimes the reading of a text requires some previous experience with another text that prepares the reader for a step upward.

One of the most dreadful mistakes we can possibly make as we study, either as students or as teachers, is to retreat before the first obstacle we face. Such a retreat makes the mistake of not accepting the responsibility presented by the task of studying, as by any other, to those who must complete it.

Studying is a demanding occupation, in the process of which we will encounter pain, pleasure, victory, defeat, doubt, and happiness. For this reason, studying requires the development of rigorous discipline, which we must consciously forge in ourselves. No one can bestow or impose such discipline on someone else; the attempt implies a total lack of knowledge about the educator's role in the development of discipline. In any case, either we are the agents of this discipline, or it becomes a mere appendage to our selves. Either we adhere to study with delight or accept it as necessity and pleasure, or it becomes a mere burden and, as such, will be abandoned at the first crossroads.

The more we accept this discipline, the more we strengthen our ability to overcome threats to it and thus to our ability to study effectively.

One such threat, for example, is allowing ourselves to not use such auxiliary tools as dictionaries, encyclopedias, and so on. We must always incorporate into our intellectual discipline the habit of consulting such tools to the extent that, without them, studying would be made difficult.

Allowing the fear of not successfully accomplishing the process of text comprehension to immobilize us evades the first battle. From there, it is just one step to accusing the author of being incomprehensible.

Another threat to serious study, a threat that is one of the most negative forms of avoiding overcoming the difficulties we face instead of taking on the difficulties of the text itself, is our *proclaiming* that we understand without, however, putting our assertion to the test.

There is no reason why I should be ashamed of not understanding something that I read. If, however, the text I cannot understand is part of a body of readings seen as essential, in order even to gain the perspective to judge whether the text is essential I must overcome my difficulties in understanding it.

It is no excess to repeat that reading, like studying, is not simply browsing leisurely over the sentences, phrases, and words of the text without any concern for knowing where they may take us.

Another threat to completing the difficult and pleasurable task of studying, a threat that results from the lack of discipline I spoke of, is the temptation always before us to abandon the printed page in the middle of reading and to glide far away in imagination. Suddenly, though we have the book physically in front of us, we are reading it only mechanically. The body is here, but the mind is on a distant tropical island. This way, it is really impossible to study.

We must be forewarned that only rarely does a text easily lend itself to the reader's curiosity. At the same time, it is not every curiosity that can penetrate the text intimately in order to study its truths, its mysteries, its weak points. Only epistemological curiosity—that which, by taking some distance from the object, "approaches" it with the intent and the pleasure of unveiling it—can begin to uncover the text, and even this fundamental curiosity is not enough. Using that curiosity to approach and examine the text, we too must give ourselves to the text, must surrender to it. In order for that to happen, we must equally avoid other fears that *scientism* has instilled in us. For example, there is the fear that our emotions, our desires, may ruin our objectivity. Whatever I know I know with my entire self: with my critical mind but also with my feelings, with my intuitions, with my emotions. What I must not do is stop at the level of emotions, of intuitions. I must place the objects of my intuition under serious, rigorous investigation; I must never disregard them.

In sum, the reading of a text is a *transaction* between the reader and the text, which mediates the encounter between reader and writer. It is a *composition* between the reader and the writer in which the reader "re-writes" the text making a determined effort not to betray the author's spirit. And it is not possible to do that without critical comprehension of the text, which in turn requires overcoming the fear of reading, which gradually takes place within the process of developing the discipline that I spoke of. Let us insist on that discipline. It has to do with reading and, for that reason, with writing as well. It is not possible to read without writing or to write without reading.

Another important aspect, and one that challenges the reader even more as "re-creator" of the text he or she reads, is that text *comprehension* is not deposited, static and immobilized, within the pages of the text, simply waiting to be uncovered by the reader. If that were the case, we could not say that reading critically is "re-writing" what one has read. That is why I spoke of reading as a *composition* between reader and writer in which the most profound significance of the text is also the creation of the reader. This point brings us to the need for reading also as a dialogic experience in which the discussion of the text undertaken by different readers clarifies, enlightens, and creates group comprehension of what has been read. Deep down, group reading brings about the emergence of different *points of view* that, as they become exposed to each other, enrich the production of text comprehension.

Of the experiences I have had with reading in and out of Brazil, I would single out as the best the ones I gained from coordinating reading groups around the text.

What I have observed is that apprehension before reading or fear itself tends to be overcome and one is free to attempt to *invent* the *meaning* of the text in addition to just discovering it.

Obviously, in preparation for group reading each participant reads individually, consults this or that auxiliary tool, and establishes this or that interpretation for certain portions of the text. The process of creating comprehension of what is being read is gradually built in the dialogue between the different points of view about the challenge, which is the author's core meaning.

As an author, I would be not just satisfied but exultant if I came to find out that this text had caused its readers to conduct the kind of committed reading that I have been insisting on throughout this book. Deep down, this must be every author's true dream—to be read, discussed, critiqued, improved, and reinvented by his or her readers.

Let us return for a moment to that aspect of critical reading according to which the reader becomes, little by little, equally the producer of the text's meaning. The more the reader makes him- or herself a real *apprehender* of the author's comprehension, all the more he or she will become a producer of text comprehension, to the extent that such comprehension becomes reader-created knowledge rather than knowledge that is deposited in the reader by the reading of the text.

When I understand an object, rather than memorizing the profile of the concept of the object, I know that object, I produce the knowledge of that object. When the reader critically achieves an understanding of the object that the author talks about, the reader *knows* the meaning of the text and becomes coauthor of that meaning. The reader then will not speak of the meaning of the text merely as someone who has heard about it. The reader has worked and reworked the meaning of the text; thus, it was not there, immobilized, waiting. Here lies the *difficulty* and the *fascination* in the act of reading.

Unfortunately, in general what has been done in schools lately is to lead students to become passive before the text. Exercises in reading interpretation tend almost to be verbal copies of the text. Children learn early on that their imagination does not work: Using their imagination is almost forbidden, a kind of sin. In addition, their cognitive abilities are challenged in a distorted manner. They are invited neither to imaginatively relive the story told in the book nor to gradually appropriate the significance of the text.

It would certainly be through the experience of recounting the story, leaving their imagination, feelings, dreams, and desires free to create, that children would end up taking a chance on producing a more complex understanding of texts.

Nothing, or almost nothing, is done toward awakening and keeping alive children's curiosity, their consciously critical reflection, so indispensable to creative reading, reading capable of unfolding into the rewriting of the text read.

This curiosity, which needs to be stimulated in the student by the teacher, decisively contributes to grasping the content of the text, which in turn is fundamental for creating the text's significance.

It is true that if the content of reading has to do with a concrete fact of social or historical reality or of biology, for example, no interpretation of the reading may deny that concrete fact. But that does not mean that the reader should memorize word-for-word what has been read and repeat the author's discourse mechanically. This would be like a "banking"[1] kind of reading, in which the reader would "eat up" the content of the author's text with the help of the "nutritionist teacher."

I insist on the undeniable importance of the educator in learning to read, inseparable from learning to write, which learners must dive into. Learning to read entails the discipline of mapping out the text thematically,[2] which must be realized not by the educator alone but also by the learners. The learners must unveil the interactions between themes within the whole of the author's discourse, and their attention must be called to the citations made within the text, as well as to their role. It is also important to underline the aesthetic moment of the author's language, his or her command of the language and vocabulary, which implies overcoming the unnecessary repetition of a given word four times on a single page of the text.

A rich exercise, which I've heard of now and again, even though it is not carried out in schools, is to enable two or three writers, of fiction or not, to speak to their student readers about how they produce their texts. They speak about how they deal with the themes or with the plots that involve their themes, how they work out their language, how they pursue the beauty of speech, of description, of leaving certain information suspended so the readers could exercise their imagination. They also speak about how they play with the transition from one time to another in their stories and, finally, about how writers read themselves and how they read other writers.

Finally, as learners experiment more and more critically with the task of reading and writing, they must grasp the social plots in which language, communication, and the production of knowledge are constituted and reconstituted.

NOTES

1. See Paulo Freire, *Pedagogy of the Oppressed* (Rio de Janeiro: Paz e Terra, 1970).

2. See Paulo Freire, *Cultural Action for Freedom and Other Works* (Rio de Janeiro: Paz e Terra).

I Came into the Teacher Training Program Because I Had No Other Options

A few years ago, when invited to speak to the participants of one of the teacher training programs in São Paulo, I heard from many of them the statement that is the title of this letter. But I also heard from many others that they had opted for the teacher training program as a way of biding their time while waiting for marriage.

I am absolutely convinced that the educational practice I have been speaking about and whose beauty and importance I have frequently alluded to must not be prepared for on the basis of such motivations as these. It is even possible that some teacher training programs may have been irresponsibly seen as "slot machines" of sorts, but that does not mean that educational practice should be viewed as some kind of awning under which people wait for the rain to let up: Waiting out a rainstorm under an awning requires no preparation or training.

Quite to the contrary, educational practice is something very serious. As teachers, we deal with people, with children, adolescents, and adults. We participate in their development. We may help them or set them back in their search. We are intrinsically connected to them in their process of discovery. Incompetence, poor preparation, and irresponsibility in our practice may contribute to their failure. But with responsibility, scientific preparation, and a taste for teaching, with seriousness and a testimony to the struggle against injustice, we can also contribute to the gradual transformation of learners into strong *presences* in the world.

In sum, even if we cannot state that an incompetent and irresponsible teacher's student is necessarily inept or that a serious and competent teacher's is automatically serious and capable, we must embrace our educational task honorably, taking our preparation for it into account rigorously.

The second reason that teachers frequently offer for opting for teacher training coincides with and reinforces the ideology that reduces the professional teacher to the status of a coddling mother.

Indispensable to teachers' struggle is the knowledge, which they must forge within themselves and which we must forge within ourselves, of the dignity and importance of their task. Without this conviction, we enter our struggle for salary and against disrespect almost defeated.

[margin note: what teachers do]

62

Obviously, recognizing the importance of our task does not mean thinking that it is the most important of all. It means recognizing that it is fundamental, in fact indispensable for social life. One must not, then, enter preparation for teaching because one lacks other opportunities, much less as something to pass the time while waiting for marriage. With such motivations, which suggest how one defines educational practice, one can only relate to the practice as a passerby waits out the rain. Thus, in most such cases, one has no reason to fight and so would not mind giving up professionalism and accepting the status of a coddling mother.

Our need to be able to fight ever more effectively for our rights, our need to feel competent and to be convinced of the social and political importance of our task, rests in the fact that, for example, the meagerness of our pay does not depend only on the economic and financial condition of the state or of private companies. These needs are also very much linked to a *colonial* comprehension of administration, of how to deal with public spending, of the hierarchy and priority of expenditures.

We must defeat arguments such as this one: "We can give, say, attorneys for the Union reasonable raises; there are only about sixty of them. We couldn't do the same for teachers; there are 20,000 of them." No. This is no argument. First, I want to know whether teachers are important or not. I want to know whether their salaries are insufficient, whether their task is indispensable or not. It is on such questions that this difficult and long struggle, which calls for patient impatience on the part of educators and political wisdom from their leadership, must be centered. It is important to fight against the colonial traditions we bring with us. It is imperative that we fight to defend the relevance of our task, a relevance that must gradually (but as quickly as possible) become incorporated within society's most general and obvious stratum of knowledge.

The more we acquiesce to being made into coddling mothers, the more society will find it strange that we go on strike and demand that we remain well behaved.

Conversely, the sooner society recognizes the relevance of our profession, the more it will support us.

It is urgent that we drum up more support in this country for public schools that are popular, effective, democratic, and happy and whose teachers are well paid, well trained, and in constant development. Never again should teachers' salaries be astronomically lower than those of the presidents and directors of government corporations, as they are today.

We must make this theme into something so national and so fundamental to Brazil's historic presence in the world in the next millennium that we can disturb the insensitive and well-behaved consciences of bureaucrats, who are immersed from head to toe in colonial ideas even when self-defined as modernizers.

It is not acceptable on the eve of the new millennium that we continue to experience the alarming quantitative and qualitative deficits that currently exist in our education. We cannot enter the new millennium with thousands of so-called lay teachers, even in the poor areas of the country, sometimes making less than the minimum wage. They are heroic people, giving, loving, intelligent people, but people treated with contempt by national oligarchies.

We cannot go on, in the last decade of this millennium, with 8 million Carlinhos and Josefas *forbidden* to have a school and with millions of others *expelled* from school while they are referred to as *dropouts*.

We are not surprised, for example, to hear that "until independence there was no educational system" in the country. Not only was there no system of public education, but cultural manifestations of any kind were prohibited. Until the arrival of the Royal Family, the establishment of print shops in the country was illegal and carried the most severe punishments.

With the Declaration of Independence, the new-born nation found itself submerged in the deepest ignorance; public education then meant no more than a few schools scattered around the provinces. Secondary education was provided through the so-called "regal classes," where a pedantic and sterile mix of Latin, Greek, rhetoric, rational and moral philosophy, and other such things was taught. Books were rare, and even the most qualified people possessed no reading habits.[1]

We must always monitor the performance of the people we vote for, whether on a local, state, or federal level; whether for mayor, senator, governor, or president; we must watch their steps, moves, decisions, statements, votes, and omissions, as well as their lack of ethics. We must hold them to their promises and evaluate them rigorously before trusting them with our votes again. If need be, we must deny them our votes and communicate to them our reasons for doing so. And perhaps most important, in doing so we must ensure, as much as possible, that we make our position public.

If we were not a country of waste, waste we learn about daily in the press and on TV, perhaps more could be done for education. We waste by poorly recycling our garbage and by showing contemptuous disrespect for public property. We waste by leaving equipment worth millions of dollars unused and exposed and by starting but not completing hospitals, day care centers, overpasses, viaducts, and huge buildings—all interrupted, soon to look like archeological sites of buried ancient civilizations. We also waste millions of dollars' worth of fruits and vegetables in the large distribution centers of the country. It might actually be worth calculating the cost of this waste to give us a sense of how much more we might be able to do for education if it didn't exist.

The arbitrariness of the powerful and the arrogance of administrators, holdovers from our colonial past, are among the explanations for the feelings of impotence and fatalism that many of us have. This arbitrariness, this arrogance, may well weaken the spirit of many teachers, who then resign themselves to being coddling mothers instead of asserting themselves as professionals; it may also explain the position of those teachers-in-training who go through the teacher training program while they "wait for marriage."

All that is really effective against this state of affairs is organized political struggle, is overcoming the corporate view of the unions, is victory over sectarian positions, is exerting pressure along with the progressive parties, not those with traditional leftist approaches but those with a postmodern agenda. All that counts is not allowing ourselves to fall into fatalism, which, even more than creating obstacles to possible solutions, reinforces the problem.

It is obvious that the problems associated with education are not just pedagogical problems. They may also be political, ethical, and financial problems.

The recently uncovered financial scandals in the social security system, according to a serious television commentator, involved enough money to build 600,000 low-income houses throughout the country.

When there is enough money for one sector but not for another, the reason can only lie within the politics of spending. There is not enough money, for instance, to make life in the slums less miserable, but there is no lack of funds to link one rich section of town to another via a majestic tunnel. This is not a technological problem; it is a political choice. Such problems have accompanied us throughout history. In 1852, when Counselor Zacarias de Vasconselos took office as head of the Province of Paraná for the first time, he called the salary of 800 réis a day absurd, as he protested against the low wages paid to elementary teachers. According to B. L. Berlinck:

> The main consequence of the lacking remuneration was that the teaching career seduced no one. That only those who had no aptitude for anything else would go into teaching was a statement repeatedly used by many province presidents. It was urgent that education be better valued by the inhabitants of Brazil. There could not be a less effective process, however, to achieve such a goal than the poor remuneration of teachers.[2]

I believe that the education workers union should add a new, long-term item to their agenda of salary increases and the improvement of working conditions in teaching: a demand for the close scrutiny of public spending policies, including the discrepancy between the salaries of elementary teachers and those of other professionals, and a demand for an analysis of all bonuses and commissions that may become incorporated in a worker's salary after any given period of time. It would be necessary to institute a serious study of salary policies that were substantively democratic rather than colonial; such a study would, on the one hand, create justice for the teaching profession and, on the other, resolve alarming inequalities.

While visiting Recife in the 1950s, Father Lebret, the founder of the economics and humanism movement, said that of all the shocking things he had seen in our midst, the most alarming was the gap in salary between the privileged and the disenfranchised. The disparity continues today. It is not possible to understand the disproportionate difference between what the president of a government corporation makes, aside from the importance of his or her work, and what an elementary teacher makes. It is ironic that the president of today's government corporation needed yesterday's elementary teacher.

It is imperative that the teaching profession in Brazil be treated with dignity so that society can begin to demand that they perform their duties effectively.

We would be naive, however, if we disregarded the need for a political struggle, the need to clarify for the public the real condition of the teaching profession, and the need to compare the salaries of different professionals and to point out the disparity between them.

It is true that education is not the ultimate lever for social transformation, but without it transformation cannot occur.

No nation can assert itself through a wild passion for knowledge without venturing emotionally into constantly reinventing itself and without creatively taking risks.

No society can assert itself without developing its culture, science, research, technology, and teaching. And all this begins in elementary school.

NOTES

1. See B. L. Berlinck, *Adverse Factors in Brazilian Education* (São Paulo: IPSIS S/A).

2. See Berlinck, *Adverse Factors in Brazilian Education*.

On the Indispensable Qualities of Progressive Teachers for Their Better Performance

I would like to make it clear that the attributes I am going to speak about, which seem to me to be indispensable to the progressive teacher, are qualities acquired gradually through practice. Furthermore, they are developed through practice in concurrence with a political decision that the educator's role is crucial. Thus the attributes I am going to speak about are not attributes that we can be born with or that can be bestowed upon us by decree or as a gift. In addition, the order in which I list them here is not intended to rank their value. They are all necessary for a progressive educational practice.

I shall start with *humility*, which here by no means carries the connotation of a lack of self-respect, of resignation, or of cowardice. On the contrary, humility requires courage, self-confidence, self-respect, and respect for others.

Humility helps us to understand this obvious truth: No one knows it all; no one is ignorant of everything. We all know something; we are all ignorant of something. Without humility, one can hardly listen with respect to those one judges to be too far below one's own level of competence. But the humility that enables one to listen even to those considered less competent should not be an act of condescension or resemble the behavior of those fulfilling a vow: "I promise the Virgin Mary that, if the problem with my eyes turns out not to be serious, I will listen to the rude and ignorant parents of my students with attention." No. None of that. Listening to all that come to us, regardless of their intellectual level, is a human duty and reveals an identification with democracy and not with elitism.

In fact, I cannot see how one could reconcile adherence to an ideal of democracy and of overcoming prejudice with a proud or arrogant posture in which one feels full of oneself. How can I listen to the other, how can I hold a dialogue, if I can only listen to myself, if I can only see myself, if nothing or no one other than myself can touch me or move me? If while humble, one does undermine oneself or accepts humiliation, one is also always ready to teach and to learn. Humility helps me avoid being entrenched in the circuit of my own truth. One of the fundamental auxiliaries of humility is *common sense*, which

Common sense!

serves to remind us that certain attitudes may lead us too close to becoming lost.

The arrogance of "You don't know who you are dealing with ...," the *conceit* of the know-it-all with an unrestrained desire to make his or her knowledge known and recognized—none of this has anything to do with the *tameness* (which is not apathy) of the humble. Humility does not flourish in people's insecurities but in the insecure security of the more aware, and thus this insecure security is one of the expressions of humility, as is uncertain certainty, unlike certainty, which is excessively sure of itself. The authoritarians' stance, in contrast, is sectarian. Theirs is the only truth, and it must be imposed on others. It is in their truth that others' salvation resides. Their knowledge "illuminates" the obscurity or the ignorance of others, who then must be subjected to the knowledge and arrogance of the authoritarian.

I will return to my analysis of authoritarianism, whether that of parents or teachers. As one might expect, authoritarianism will at times cause children and students to adopt *rebellious* positions, defiant of any limit, discipline, or authority. But it will also lead to apathy, excessive obedience, uncritical conformity, lack of resistance against authoritarian discourse, self-abnegation, and fear of freedom.

In saying that authoritarianism may generate various types of reactions, I understand that on a human level things do not happen so *mechanically* and happily. Thus it is possible that certain children will go through the rigors of arbitrariness unscathed, which does not give us the license to gamble on that possibility and fail to make an effort to become less authoritarian. And if we can't make that effort for our dream for democracy, we should make it out of respect for beings in development, our children and our students.

But to the humility with which teachers perform and relate to their students, another quality needs to be added: *lovingness*, without which their work would lose its meaning. And here I mean lovingness not only toward the students but also toward the very process of teaching. I must confess, not meaning to cavil, that I do not believe educators can survive the negativities of their trade without some sort of "armed love," as the poet Tiago de Melo would say. Without it they could not survive all the injustice or the government's contempt, which is expressed in the shameful wages and the arbitrary treatment of teachers, not coddling mothers, who take a stand, who participate in protest activities through their union, who are punished, and who yet remain devoted to their work with students.

It is indeed necessary, however, that this love be an "armed love," the fighting love of those convinced of the right and the duty to fight, to denounce, and to announce. It is this form of love that is indispensable to the progressive educator and that we must all learn.

It so happens, however, that this lovingness I speak about, the dream for which I fight and for whose realization I constantly prepare myself, demands that I invent in myself, in my social experience, another quality: *courage*, to fight and to love.

Courage, as a virtue, is not something I can find outside myself. Because it comprises the conquering of my fears, it implies fear.

First of all, in speaking about fear we must make sure that we are speaking of something very concrete. In other words, fear is not an abstraction. Second, we must make sure that we understand that we are speaking of something very normal. And, when we speak about fear, we are faced with the need to be very clear of our choices, and that requires certain concrete procedures and practices, which are the very experiences that cause fear.

To the extent that I become clearer about my choices and my dreams, which are substantively political and attributively pedagogical, and to the extent that I recognize that though an educator I am also a political agent, I can better understand why I fear and realize how far we still have to go to improve our democracy. I also understand that as we put into practice an education that critically provokes the learner's consciousness, we are necessarily working against myths that deform us. As we confront such myths, we also face the dominant power because those myths are nothing but the expression of this power, of its ideology.

When we are faced with concrete fears, such as that of losing our jobs or of not being promoted, we feel the need to set certain limits to our fear. Before anything else, we begin to recognize that fear is a manifestation of our being alive. I do not need to hide my fears. But I must not allow my fears to immobilize me. If I am secure in my political dream, having tactics that may lessen my risk, I must go on with the fight. Hence the need to be in control of my fear, to *educate* my fear, from which is finally born my courage.[1] Thus I must neither, on the one hand, deny my fears nor, on the other, surrender myself to them. Instead, I must control them, for it is in the very exercise of this control that my necessary courage is shared.

That is why though there may be fear without courage, the fear that devastates and paralyzes us, there may never be courage without fear, that which "speaks" of our humanness as we manage to limit, subject, and control it.

Tolerance is another virtue. Without it no serious pedagogical work is possible; without it no authentic democratic experience is viable; without it all progressive educational practice denies itself. Tolerance is not, however, the irresponsible position of those who play the game of make-believe.

Being tolerant does not mean acquiescing to the intolerable; it does not mean covering up disrespect; it does not mean coddling the aggressor or disguising aggression. Tolerance is the virtue that teaches us to live with the different. It teaches us to learn from and respect the different.

On an initial level, tolerance may almos͏ favor, as if being tolerant were a courte way of accepting, of *tolerating*, the not-qui͏ ence of one's opposite, a civilized way of permittin͏g existence that might seem repugnant. That, however, is hypocrisy, not tolerance. Hypocrisy is a defect; it is degradation. Tolerance is a virtue. Thus if I live tolerance, I should embrace it. I must experience it as something that makes me coherent first with my historical being, inconclusive as that may sound, and second with my democratic political choice. I cannot see how one might be democratic without experiencing tolerance, coexistence with the different, as a fundamental principle.

No one can learn tolerance in a climate of irresponsibility, which does not produce democracy. The act of tolerating requires a climate in which limits may be established, in which there are principles to be respected. That is why tolerance is not coexistence with the intolerable. Under an authoritarian regime, in which authority is abused, or a permissive one, in which freedom is not limited, one can hardly learn tolerance. Tolerance requires respect, discipline, and ethics. The authoritarian, filled with sexual, racial, and class prejudices, can never become tolerant without first overcoming his or her prejudices. That is why a bigot's *progressive* discourse, which contrasts with his or her practice, is a false discourse. That is also why those who embrace scientism are equally intolerant, because they take science for the *ultimate truth*, outside of which nothing counts, believing that only science can provide certainty. Those immersed in scientism cannot be tolerant, though that fact should not discredit science.

I would also like to add *decisiveness, security,* the tension between *patience and impatience,* and *joy of living* to the group of qualities to be nourished in ourselves if we are to be progressive educators.

An educator's ability to make decisions is absolutely necessary to his or her educational work. It is by demonstrating an ability to make decisions that an educator teaches the difficult virtue of decisiveness. Making decisions is difficult to the extent that it signifies breaking free to choose. No one ever decides anything without making a trade-off, weighing one thing against another, one point against another, one person against another. Thus every choice that follows a particular decision calls for careful evaluation in comparing and opting for one of the possible sides, persons, or positions. It is evaluation, with all its implications, that helps us to finally make choices.

Decision making is rupture and is not always an easy experience. But it is not possible to exist without rupturing, no matter how hard it may be.

One of the deficiencies that an educator may possess is an inability to make decisions. Such *indecision* is perceived by learners as either moral weakness or professional incompetence. Democratic educators must not nullify themselves in the name of being democratic. On the contrary, although they cannot take sole responsibility for the lives of their students, they must not, in the name of democracy, evade the responsibility of making decisions. At the same time, they must not be arbitrary in their decisions. Setting an example, as an authority figure, of not taking responsibility for one's duties, of allowing oneself to fall into permissiveness, is even more somber a fate for a teacher than abusing authority.

There are plenty of occasions when a good democracy-oriented pedagogical example is to make the decision in question with the students, after analyzing the problem. Other times, when the decision to be made is within the scope of the educator's expertise, there is no reason not to take action, to be negligent.

Indecision reveals a lack of confidence; but confidence is indispensable for anyone with responsibilities in government, whether of a class, a family, an institution, a company, or the state.

Security, confidence, on the other hand, requires scientific competence, political clarity, and ethical integrity.

One cannot be secure in one's actions without knowing how to support those actions scientifically, without at least some idea of what one does, why, and to what end. The same is true of allegiance: One must know whom or what one is for or against. Nor can one be secure in one's actions without being moved by them, or if one hurts the dignity of others, exposing them to embarrassing situations. Such ethical irresponsibility and cynicism show an inability to live up to the educator's task, which demands critically disciplined performance with which to challenge learners. On the one hand, such discipline reflects the educator's competence, as it is gradually revealed to the learners, discreetly and humbly, without arrogant outbursts; on the other, it affects the balance with which the educator exercises authority— secure, lucid, and determined.

None of this, however, can be realized if an educator lacks a taste for permanently seeking justice. No one can prevent a teacher from liking one student more than another, for any number of reasons. That is a teacher's right. What a teacher must not do is disregard the rights of the other students in favoring one student.

There is another fundamental quality that the progressive educator must not lack: He or she must exercise wisdom in experiencing the tension between *patience* and *impatience*. Neither *patience* nor *impatience* alone is what is called for. Patience alone may bring the educator to a position of resignation, of permissiveness, that denies the educator's democratic dream. Unaccompanied patience may lead to immobility, to inactivity. Conversely, impatience alone may lead the educator to blind activism, to action for its own sake, to a practice that does not respect the necessary relationship between tactics and strategy. Isolated patience tends to hinder the attainment of objectives central to the educator's practice, making it soft and ineffectual. Untempered impatience threatens the success of one's practice, which becomes lost in the arrogance of judging oneself the owner of history. Patience alone consumes itself in mere prattle; impatience alone consumes itself in irresponsible activism.

Virtue, then, does not lie in experiencing either without the other but, rather, in living the permanent tension between the two. The educator must live and work impatiently patiently, never surrendering entirely to either.

Alongside this harmonious, balanced way of being and working there must figure another quality, which I have been calling *verbal parsimony*. Verbal parsimony is implied in the assumption of patience-impatience. Those who live impatient patience will rarely lose control over their words; they will rarely exceed the limits of considered yet energetic discourse. Those who predominantly live patience alone stifle their legitimate anger, which then is expressed through weak and resigned discourse. Those, on the other hand, who are all uncontrolled impatience tend toward lack of restraint in discourse. The patient person's discourse is always *well-behaved*, whereas that of the impatient person generally goes beyond what reality itself could withstand.

Both of these kinds of discourse, the overly controlled as well as the undisciplined, contribute to the preservation of the status quo. The first falls short of the demands of the status quo; the second surpasses its limits.

The benevolent classroom discourse and practice of those who are only patient suggest to learners that anything, or almost anything, goes. There is in the air a sense of a nearly infinite patience. Nervous, arrogant, uncontrolled, unrealistic, unrestrained discourse will find itself immersed in inconsequence and irresponsibility.

In no way do these discourses contribute to the learners' education.

There are also those who are excessively restrained in their discourse but who once in a while lose control. From absolute patience, they leap unexpectedly into uncontainable impatience, creating a climate of insecurity for everyone around them, always with terrible effects.

Countless mothers and fathers behave so. Today their words and their actions are permissive, but they transform tomorrow into the opposite, a universe of authoritarian discourse and orders, which not only leaves their sons and daughters appalled but, above all, makes them insecure. Such immoderate parental behavior limits children's emotional balance, which they need to grow up. Loving is not enough; one must know how to love.

Though I recognize that these reflections on qualities are incomplete, I would also like to briefly discuss *joy of living* as a fundamental virtue for democratic educational practice.

By completely giving myself to life rather than to death—without meaning either to deny death or to mythicize life—I can free myself to surrender to the joy of living, without having to hide the reasons for sadness in life, which prepares me to stimulate and champion joy in the school.

Whether or not we are willing to overcome slips or inconsistencies, by living humility, lovingness, courage, tolerance, competence, decisiveness, patience-impatience, and verbal parsimony, we contribute to creating a happy, joyful school. We forge a school-adventure, a school that marches on, that is not afraid of the risks, and that rejects immobility. It is a school that thinks, that participates, that creates, that speaks, that loves, that guesses, that passionately embraces and says *yes* to life. It is not a school that quiets down and quits.

Indeed the easy way out in dealing with the obstacles posed by governmental contempt and the arbitrariness of antidemocratic authorities is the fatalist resignation in which many of us find ourselves.

"What can I do? Whether they call me *teacher* or coddling mother, I am still underpaid, disregarded, and uncared for. Well, so be it." In reality, this is the most convenient position, but it is also the position of someone who quits the struggle, who quits history. It is the position of those who renounce conflict, the lack of which undermines the dignity of life. There may not be life or human existence without struggle and conflict. Conflict[2] shares in our conscience. Denying conflict, we ignore even the most mundane aspects of our vital and social experience. Trying to escape conflict, we preserve the status quo.

Thus I can see no alternative for educators to unity within the diversity of their interests in defending their rights. Such rights include the right to freedom in teaching, the right to speak, the right to better conditions for pedagogical work, the right to paid sabbaticals for continuing education, the right to be coherent, the right to criticize the authorities without fear of retaliation (which entails the duty to criticize truthfully), the right to the duty to be serious and coherent and to not have to lie to survive.

We must fight so that these rights are not just recognized but respected and implemented. At times we may need to fight side by side with the unions; at other times we may need to fight against them, if their leadership is sectarian, whether right or left. At other times we also need to fight as a progressive administration against the devilish anger of the obsolete; of the traditionalists, some of whom judge themselves progressive; and of the neoliberals, who see themselves as the culmination of history.

NOTES

1. See Paulo Freire and Ira Shor, *Medo e Ousadia, o Cotidiano do Professor* (Rio de Janeiro: Paz e Terra, 1987).

2. See Moacir Gadotti, Paulo Freire, and Sergio Guimarães, *Pedagogy: Dialogue and Conflict* (Rio de Janeiro: Cortez, 1989).

The First Day of School

I would like now to focus, not permissively but with true spontaneity, on a series of problems that are faced not only by novice teachers but also by more experienced ones and that teachers need to respond to. Yet it is not as if the thought even crosses my mind, as I write this letter, that I might have *the answers* to all these problems and difficulties I will point out. I do feel, however, that I may have some useful suggestions to make, the result of my experience and systematic knowledge. If, as I wrote this letter, or this entire book, I had become immersed in the notion that I might have the whole truth about the various topics addressed, I would be betraying my own understanding of the process of knowledge production as social, as open-ended, as unfolding. On the other hand, if I felt I had nothing to contribute to the professional development of those in preparation for teaching, even those who may already be involved in educational practice, I should not have written this book, for it would be useless.

I do not have *the truth;* this book contains *truths,* and my dream is that as those truths challenge or question the positions taken by the book's readers, they may engage those readers in a critical dialogue in which their practice, their understanding of the theory that informs that practice, and my analysis will serve as a frame of reference. I have never written a book intending for its content to be swallowed by readers. That is why in a previous letter I insisted so much on the reader's role, which he or she may not refuse, as a producer of textual meaning.

I would also like to clarify, as I wander around aspects of the different topics I will address, that in my comings and goings about these topics I shall return to some previously mentioned points. I shall try my best, however, to elucidate rather than repeat.

I will begin by commenting on the situation of a teacher who, for the first time, becomes completely exposed to students.

That first day will hardly be devoid of insecurities, of shyness, or of inhibition, especially if the teacher in question does not just think he or she is insecure but is indeed so, if he or she *fears* not being able to perform the work or to work around difficulties. Deep down, all of a sudden, the concrete situation the teacher is faced with in the classroom seems to have nothing to do with the theories that have been taught. Perhaps there is some relationship between previously studied theory and the concrete situation, but the teacher, overwhelmed with insecurity, is left shaken, confused, not knowing how to decide.

Indeed, fear is a right, but one to which corresponds the duty of educating it, of facing it and overcoming it. Facing a fear, not running away from it, implies analyzing its reasons for being and gauging the relationship between what causes it and our ability to respond. Facing a fear is not hiding it; this is the only way to conquer it.

Throughout my life I have never lost anything by exposing myself and my feelings, obviously within certain limits. In a situation like this, I believe the best course of action is to face up to one's feelings, rather than falsely expressing confidence through a discourse that, so untrue, reveals one's weakness. The best is to tell the learners, in a demonstration of being human and limited, how one feels at the time. It is to speak to them about the very right to fear, which cannot be denied to the educator. Teachers have as much right to fear as learners do. The educator is not invulnerable. He or she is as human as the learner. An inability to fight to overcome fear would speak against one's qualification as an educator, but the fact that one might experience fear does not. The fear of performing on the first day of class, often before experienced students who can guess the insecurity of a novice teacher, is completely natural.

By speaking about their fears or insecurities, educators move gradually toward overcoming them, and at the same time they gradually win the confidence of learners. This way, instead of trying to hide fear with *authoritarian* disguises easily recognized by learners, teachers humbly admit it. By speaking of their feelings, they accept themselves as persons, they testify to their desire to learn with the learners. It is obvious that this necessary posture on the part of educators, before their fears and before learners, requires the peace of mind brought by humility. But it also requires deep trust—not naive but critical trust—in people and a coherently experienced choice for democracy. Elitist and authoritarian educators, like those for whom democracy seems to be deteriorating when the popular classes begin to flood the streets with protest, never understand the humility of facing up to fear as anything other than cowardice. In reality, facing a fear is the first step in turning it into *courage*.

Another fundamental aspect related to the early experiences of novice teachers, one that teacher training programs should pay the closest attention to if they don't already, is teachers' preparation for "reading" a class of students as if it were a *text* to be decoded, comprehended.

The novice teacher must be attentive to everything, even to the most innocent movements on the part of the students: the restlessness of their bodies, a surprised gaze, or a more or less aggressive reaction on the part of this or that student.

When inexperienced middle-class teachers take teaching positions in peripheral areas of the city, class-specific tastes, values, language, discourse, syntax, semantics, everything about the students may seem contradictory to the point of being shocking and frightening. It is necessary, however, that teachers understand that the students' syntax; their manners, tastes, and ways of addressing teachers and colleagues; and the rules governing their fighting and playing among themselves are all part of their *cultural identity*, which never lacks an element of class. All that has to be accepted. Only as learners recognize themselves democratically and see that their right to say "I be" is respected will they become able to learn the dominant grammatical reasons why they should say "I am."

[handwritten margin note: cultural identity]

[handwritten margin note: understanding who they are]

A good exercise in the intellectual discipline required for "reading" the class as if it were a text would be for teachers to develop the habit, more out of pleasure than mere obligation, of taking daily notes recording the students' behavioral reactions, their phrases and their meanings, and their gestures of tenderness or refusal. And why not suggest to learners, perhaps as a game, that they too, as a function of their command of language, observe the gestures, language, humor, and behavior of teachers and colleagues? Perhaps every two weeks there could be some sort of evaluative seminar at which certain conclusions would be drawn for more in-depth analysis and to be put into practice.

If four teachers in one school were able to carry out such a project with their students, we can only imagine how much growth in all areas might result between teachers and students.

An important observation should be made here. Just as in order to read texts we need such auxiliary tools as dictionaries or encyclopedias, the reading of classes as texts also requires tools that can be easily used. It is necessary, for example, to *observe* well, to *compare* well, to *infer* well, to *imagine* well, to *free one's sensibilities* well, and to believe others, without believing too much what one may think about others. One must exercise one's ability to *observe* by recording what is observed. But recording should not be limited to the dutiful description of what takes place from one's own perspective. It also implies taking the risk of making critical and evaluative observations without giving such observations airs of certainty. All such material should be in constant analysis by the teacher who produces it, as well as by his or her students. At every step of the way, in studying and restudying the data collected, there should be dialogue with students, which should result in correction as well as ratification. This way, the "class as a text" gradually also builds an improved understanding of itself, with the educator's participation. And producing a new understanding of itself, which implies reproducing the previous understanding, may lead the class to the production of new knowledge about itself, through a better understanding of its previous knowledge.

We should not fear our feelings, emotions, or desires; we should deal with them with the same respect that we devote ourselves to a cognitive practice that integrates them. We should be cautioned about and open to the *relationships* between facts, data, and the objects of a comprehension of reality. None of that is outside the educator's task in the context of his or her reading of the class, which serves as evidence that the educator's practice is not limited to mechanically teaching content. It also serves as evidence that the necessary teaching of content should not be devoid of critical knowledge about the social, cultural, and economic conditions within the learners' context.

It is this critical understanding of the learners' context that can explain the dramatic, indeed the tragic, existence of a countless number of subordinated students, a tragic existence in which they experience death much more closely than life, in which life indeed becomes little more than an excuse to die.

"Do you usually dream?" a television reporter once asked a ten-year-old child worker in the interior of São Paulo. "No," said the child, surprised at the question, "I only have nightmares."

The affective existence of countless numbers of children is rotten, almost crushed, like broken glass. That is the reason why they need teachers who are professionally competent and loving, rather than just coddling mothers.

Teachers must not be afraid of tenderness, must not close themselves to the affective neediness of beings who are indeed kept from being. Only the poorly loved ones can understand teaching as a trade for the insensitive, so filled with *rationalism* that they become empty of life or feeling.

I believe, on the contrary, that sensitivity to the pain imposed on the Brazilian popular classes by the evil contempt with which they are treated pushes us forward and motivates us to fight politically for the radical transformation of the world.

None of this is easily accomplished, and I would not like to leave readers with the impression that wanting is enough to change the world. Desire is fundamental, but it is not enough. It is also necessary to know how to want, to learn how to want, which implies learning how to fight politically with tactics adequate to our strategic dreams. What does not seem possible to me is to do nothing or to do too little before the terrible contradictions that afflict us. And as far as making the world, our world, a better place goes, there is no need to distinguish between modest or extravagant actions. Anything that can be done with competence, loyalty, clarity, perseverance, anything that strengthens the fight against the powers of non-love, selfishness, and evil, is equally important. In this sense, the role of a union leader in a factory, explaining, in front of the company's gates at dawn, the reasons for a strike in progress is as valid as that of a teacher in a peripheral school who speaks to his or her students about their right to defend their cultural identity. Both the union leader in the factory and the teacher at school have a great deal to do.

It is imperative that I say that I have no intention of reducing progressive educational practice to a mere political, partisan effort. What I mean to say is that we cannot teach content as if that were all there is.

Teachers must give creative wings to their imaginations, obviously in disciplined fashion. From the very first day of class, they must demonstrate to students the importance of imagination for life. Imagination helps curiosity and inventiveness, just as it enhances adventure, without which we cannot create. I speak here of imagination that is naturally free, flying, walking, or running freely. Such imagination should be present in every movement of our bodies, in dance, in rhythm, in drawing and in writing, even in the early stages when writing is in fact *prewriting*—scribbling. It should be part of speech, present in the telling and retelling of stories produced within the learners' culture. The imagination that takes us to possible and impossible dreams is always necessary. It is necessary to stimulate the learners' imagination, to use it in "blueprinting" the school they dream of. Why not put into practice right in the classroom the school they dream about? Why not, in discussing imagination projects, point out to students the concrete obstacles to attaining imagination, obstacles that, for the time being, are not easily overcome? Why not emphasize their right to imagine, to dream, and to fight for that dream? The imagination devoted to the possible and necessary dream of freedom has to confront the reactionary forces who feel that freedom is exclusively for them. Finally, it is important to make it clear that imagination is not an exercise for those detached from reality, those who live in the air. On the contrary, when we imagine something, we do it necessarily conditioned by a lack in our concrete reality. When children imagine free and happy schools, it is because their real schools deny them freedom and happiness.

Up until the time I left Recife, I read various volumes of local popular poetry, in which the poets specifically explore the deficiencies of their environments.

I will never forget one of those books' description of a giant loaf of corn bread that the entire population of a district feasted upon. That was not an example of wild imagination but, rather, evidence of the insanity that is a famished population. The dream shaped so abundantly in poetry was the expression of a concrete need.

Let us now consider a class of students who, with a coordinating, sensitive, and intelligent teacher, imagined in dialogue a system of disciplinary principles for a certain group within the class. That system might even include some excessively strict principles. Such a "make-believe" constitution would be put into effect based on one fundamental principle: the possibility of changing the rules through majority vote. There would naturally be mechanisms to enforce the rules, but all would be done democratically. In a society such as ours, of robust authoritarian tradition, it is relevant and important that we seek democratic pathways leading to the creation of limits to both freedom and authority so we can avoid the permissiveness that leads us to a "go with the flow" mentality or to all-powerful absolutism.

Issues of sociability, imagination, feelings, desires, fear, courage, love, hate, raw anger, sexuality, and so on lead us to the need to "read" our bodies as if they were texts, through the interrelations that make up their whole.

There is the need for an interdisciplinary reading of bodies with students, for breaking away from dichotomies, ruptures that are enviable and deforming.

My presence *in* the world, *with* the world, and *with* other people implies my complete knowledge of myself. And the better I understand myself in such completeness, the more it will be possible for me to make history, knowing that I too am made by history. As I become this creative agent of history at the same time that I am reinvented by history, as I exist in the world and with the world, the reading of my body, as well as that of other bodies, implies the reading of space.[1] In this sense, the class's space, the space of the classroom, stretching out into the play yard and into the surrounding areas of the entire school, which houses the fears, illusions, desires, and dreams of teachers and learners, must also constitute an object of this reading by teachers and students, as emphasized by Madalena Freire Weffort.[2]

One can really perceive the absurdity of the authoritarianism that claims that all these spaces belong to the educational authorities, to teachers. (This claim of ownership is not based on adulthood, since cooks, janitors, security guards, and cleaning staff are also adults but, because they are mere servers within school space, that space does not belong to them any more than it belongs to students.) It is as if learners were *in* the space but not *with the space.*

The progressive, democratic, happy, and capable school must rethink all these relationships between conscious body and world. We must redefine our understanding of world; though it is historically produced in the world, this understanding is also produced by conscious bodies in their interactions with the world. I believe the result of this comprehension is a new understanding of teaching and learning, and of discovery; and in considering that concept, we must remember the works of Lev Vygotsky.

NOTES

1. See Maurice Merleau-Ponty, *Phenomenology of Perception*, translated by Colin Smith (New York: Routledge, 1962).

2. In conversation with the author.

On the Relationship Between the Educator and the Learners

I now focus on an analysis of the relationship between educator and learners, a relationship that involves the questions of teaching, of learning, of the knowing-teaching-learning process, of authority, of freedom, of reading, of writing, of the virtues of the educator, and of the cultural identity of the learners and the respect that must be paid to it.

I consider testimony to be a coherent and permanent "discourse" of the progressive educator. I will try to think of testimony as the best way to call learners' attention to the validity that is proposed for the attainment of what is valued, for resolve in the struggle, with the goal of overcoming difficulties. An educational practice in which there is no coherent relationship between what educators say and what they do is a disaster.

What can be expected from teachers who protest against the administration's restrictions on their freedom to teach but who at the same time dishonorably restrict the freedom of the learners? Fortunately, on the human level, no mechanical explanation elucidates anything. We cannot declare that the students of such an educator will necessarily become apathetic or live in permanent rebellion. But it would be much better for them if they were not subjected to such a discrepancy between what is said and what is done. And of the testimony of saying and the testimony of doing, the stronger is doing because it has or can have immediate effects. The worst thing, however, for the training of the learner is that in the face of the contradiction between words and deeds, the learner tends not to believe what the educator says. If the educator makes a statement, the learner waits for the next action to detect the next contradiction. And this destroys the image that educators construct of themselves and reveal to the learners.

Children are extremely sensitive to teachers who do exactly the opposite of what they say. The saying "Do what I say, and not what I do" is an almost vain attempt to remedy the contradiction and the incoherence—"Almost vain" because what is said and is being contradicted by what is done is not always completely oppressed. What is said has, at times, such a force in itself that it defends itself against the hypocrisy of one who while saying it does the opposite. But exactly because it is only being said and not lived, it loses much of its force. He who sees the contradiction occurring could well say to himself: "If what is being proclaimed but, at the same time, so strongly denied in practice were really a good thing, it would not only be said but lived."

One of the worst things in all this is the breakdown of the relationship between educator and learners.

And what can be said of the teachers who never assume authority in the classroom, who constantly show weakness, doubt, and insecurity in their relationship with the learners?

I remember myself as an adolescent, and how much it hurt me to see the disrespect that one of our teachers left himself open to, being the object of abuse by most of the students because he had no way of imposing order on the class. His class was the second of the morning, and, already beaten down, he came into the room where the young people with a mean streak waited to punish and mistreat him. On finishing this travesty of the class, he could not turn his back to the students and walk to the door. The boisterous jeers would fall on him, heavy and arresting, and this must have petrified him. From the corner of the room where I sat I saw him, pale, belittled, shrinking toward the door. He would open it quickly and disappear, wrapped in his unsustaining weakness.

I remember from my adolescence the image of that weak, defenseless, pale man who carried with him the fear of the boys who made his weakness a plaything, together with the fear of losing his job, in the fear generated by those kids.

While I witnessed the destruction of his authority, I, who dreamed of becoming a teacher, promised myself that I would never allow myself to be subjected to such a denial of my being, neither by the all-powerful authoritarian, the arrogant teacher who always has the last word, nor by the insecurity and complete lack of presence and power exhibited by that teacher.

Another testimony that should not be missing from our relationship with students is the testimony of our constant commitment to justice, liberty, and individual rights, of our dedication to defending the weakest when they are subjected to the exploitation of the strongest. It is important, also, in this daily task, to show students that there is beauty in the ethical struggle. Ethics and aesthetics are intimately tied together. Do not say, however, that in areas of immense poverty, of dire need, these things cannot be accomplished. The experiences that teacher Madalena Freire Weffort lived personally for three years in a slum in São Paulo, in which, more than in any other context, she fully became an educator and a pedagogue (who has a political understanding of the task of teaching), were experiences in which this was possible. She is preparing a book about her experiences in a context lacking everything that our appreciation and our knowledge of class considers indispensable but full of many other elements that our knowledge of class scorns. In this text, she will certainly tell and analyze the story of little Carla, whom I quoted in one of my papers[1] and whose story is as follows: "Circling around the school, wandering in the streets of the neighborhood, half naked, with a face so dirty that it hid her beauty, an object of mockery by other children and adults as well, she wandered around as a lost soul, and what was worse, she was lost from herself, a kind of nobody's little girl."

One day, Madalena said, the little girl's grandmother approached her to ask that her granddaughter be allowed into the school, saying also that they couldn't pay the almost token tuition set by the school administration.

"I don't think there will be a problem about the payment. I do, however, have a requirement before accepting little Carla: that she come here to me clean, bathed, with at least some clothes. And that she come every day and not just tomorrow," said Madalena. The grandmother accepted this and promised that she would do what was asked. The next day Carla came to class completely changed. Clean, with a pretty face, her features uncovered, confident.

Cleanliness, a face free of dirt, highlighted Carla's presence in the classroom. She began to have confidence in herself. The grandmother likewise began to believe not only in Carla but in herself as well. Little Carla discovered herself; the grandmother rediscovered herself.

A naive bystander would say that the educator's intervention had been somewhat bourgeois, elitist, alienated— after all, how can one require that a child of the slums come to school bathed?

Madalena, in truth, fulfilled her duty as a progressive educator. Her intervention made it possible for the child and the grandmother to conquer a space—that of their dignity, in the respect of others. Tomorrow it will also be easier for Carla to recognize herself as a member of an entire class, as a worker, in search of a brighter future.

Without the democratic intervention of the educator, there is no progressive education.

So, just as it was possible for the teacher to intervene in the questions of hygiene that extend to the beauty of the body and of the world, from which resulted Carla's discovery and her grandmother's rediscovery, there is no reason why one cannot intervene in the problems that I referred to earlier.

I believe that the basic question that we educators, quite lucid and ever more competent, should confront is that our relationship with the learners is one of the roads that we can take to intervene in reality over both the short and the long term. In this sense (and not only in this sense but in others as well), our relationship with the learners demands that we respect them and demands equally that we be aware of the concrete conditions of their world, the conditions that shape them. To try to know the reality that our students live is a task that the educational practice imposes on us: Without this, we have no access to the way they think, so only with great difficulty can we perceive what and how they know.

It is my conviction that there are no themes or values of which one cannot speak, no areas in which one must be silent. We can talk about everything, and we can give testimony about everything. The language that we use to talk about this or that and the way we give testimony are, nevertheless, influenced by the social, cultural, and historical conditions of the context in which we speak and testify. It should be said that they are conditioned by the culture of the class, by the reality of those with whom and to whom we speak and testify.

Let us emphasize the importance of the testimony of sobriety, of discipline in doing things, of discipline in study; of the testimony in the care of the body, of the health; of the testimony in the honor with which educators carry out their work, in the hope with which they struggle for their rights, in the persistence with which they struggle against arbitrary judgment. The educators of this country have much besides content to teach to boys and girls, no matter from what social class they come. They have much to teach through the example of fighting for the fundamental changes that we need, of fighting against authoritarianism and in favor of democracy. None of this is easy, but it all constitutes one of the battlefronts of the great struggle for a profound transformation of Brazilian society. Progressive educators need to convince themselves that they are not only teachers—this doesn't exist—not only teaching specialists. We are political militants because we are teachers.

Our job is not exhausted in the teaching of math, geography, syntax, history. Our job implies that we teach these subjects with sobriety and competence, but it also requires our involvement in and dedication to overcoming social injustice.

It is necessary to unmask the ideology of a certain neoliberal discourse, called at times the "modernizing discourse," that, speaking about the present moment in history, tries to convince us that life is just like this: The most capable organize the world, they produce; the least capable, survive.[2] And, they say, "this conversation of dreams, of utopia, of radical change" only gets in the way of the tireless hard work of those who really do produce; we should let them work in peace without the problems that our dreamy discourse causes, and one day there will be a lot left over to be distributed.

This unacceptable discourse against hope, utopia, and dreams defends the preservation of a society like ours, a society that functions for a third of its population, as if it were possible to bear an inappropriate size for a long time. It seems to me that the new age brings us the death of sectarianism but the birth of radicalism.[3] The sectarian positions in which we pretend to be the people who know the truth, a truth that cannot be contested—positions that are still taken in the name of democracy—have less and less to do with a new age. In this sense, the progressive parties don't have much choice. Either they re-create and reinvent themselves in the radicalism of their dreams, or, dedicated to castrating sectarianisms, they perish, suffocated in Stalinist ideology. They become again, or they continue to be, old, leftist parties, without a soul, doomed to die of cold. And it's a pity that this risk exists.

Let's go back to the relationship between educators and learners, to the strength and importance in learners' preparation of educators' testimony and of the radicalism with which they act, with which they decide. In their testimony, they can and should see again, without difficulty, the position that they assumed in the face of the new elements that made them change. And their testimony will be so much more effective as they lucidly and objectively make clear to the learners

1. that changing one's position is legitimate, and
2. the reasons that made them change.

I do not think that educators need to be perfect saints. It is exactly as human beings, with their virtues and faults, that they should bear witness to the struggle for sobriety, for freedom, for the creation of the indispensable discipline of study, in which process educators must take part as auxiliaries since it is the task of learners to generate discipline in themselves.

Once educators begin the testimonial process, little by little learners begin doing it as well. This effective participation by learners is a sign that the testimony by educators is working. It is possible, however, for some learners to pretend to test educators to see if they are consistent or not. It would be a disaster if, in this case, educators reacted badly to the challenge. In reality, the majority of the learners that test teachers do so anxiously, hoping that they are not being fooled. They want educators to confirm that their testimony is true. In testing them, the learners really don't want to see them fail. But there are also those who provoke because they want educators to fail.

One of the mistakes made by educators, a mistake generated by an exorbitant self-esteem that does not make them very humble, is to feel hurt by the behavior of the learners, that is, to fail to admit that anyone could doubt them.

On the contrary, it is good to admit humbly that we are all human beings and, as such, imperfect. We are not perfect and infallible.

I remember an experience that I had, when I was recently returned from exile, with a group of graduate students from the Pontiff Catholic University of São Paulo.

On the first day of class, talking about how I saw the process of our meetings, I mentioned that I would like them to be open, democratic, free, that I would like our meetings to be such that we could exercise the right to our curiosity, the right to ask, to disagree, to criticize.

One student said aggressively: "I would like to attend the course attentively—I will not miss a single meeting— to see if the dialogue you spoke of really will be realized."

When she finished, I made a brief comment about her right to doubt me, as well as her right to express her doubts publicly. It was my duty to prove, throughout the semester, that I was true to my discourse.

In fact, the young woman never missed a meeting. She participated in all of them, she revealed her authoritarian positions, which must have been the basis for her rejection of my past and my present antigovernment militancy. We never came to a meeting of the minds, but we maintained a climate of mutual respect until the end.

In the case of this woman, what really interested her was that I would misspeak myself the first day. I did not do so. I don't get offended if students put me to the test. I don't feel infallible. I know that I am imperfect. What irritates me is being accused of dishonesty. That is unfounded criticism, and there is a lack of ethics in the accusations.

In sum, the relationship between educators and learners is complex, fundamental, and difficult; it is a relationship about which we should think constantly. How nice it would be, nevertheless, if we tried to create the habit of evaluating it or of evaluating ourselves in it while we were educators and learners also.

How nice it would be, really, if we set aside a regular time to work with learners, every two days, in which we would dedicate ourselves to the critical analysis of our language, of our practice. We would learn and we would teach together a tool indispensable to the act of studying:

the registration of facts and of what is tied to them. The act of registering leads us to observe, compare, and select, to establish relationships between facts and things. Educators and learners would commit themselves to daily jotting down the moments that had challenged them most positively or negatively from one meeting to the next.

I am convinced, moreover, that such a preparatory experience could be done, with a level of challenge appropriate to the age of the children, among those who do not yet write. To ask them to talk about how they experience their days in school would make it possible for them to engage in an education of the senses. It would demand that they pay attention to, observe, and select facts. With this we would also develop their verbal skills, which, since they contain the next stage, that of writing, should never be isolated. The children who speak in ordinary interpersonal situations are the children who write. If they don't write, their ability to write is impeded, and, only in exceptional cases, it becomes impossible for them.

When I was secretary of education of the city of São Paulo, I had an experience that I will never forget. In two city schools, I conversed for two hours with fifty fifth-grade students one afternoon and again with forty the following day. The central topic of the meetings was how the young people saw their school and what kind of school they would like to have, how they saw themselves, and how they saw the teachers.

As soon as we began to work, in the first meeting, one of the young people asked me: "Paulo, what do you think of a teacher that makes a student stand up, 'sniffing' the wall, as if he had done something wrong, as I admit that he did?" I responded: "I think the teacher made a mistake."

"What would you do if you found a teacher doing this?"

"I hope," I said, "that you and your colleagues do not assume that I should do the same with the teacher. This would be a foolish act, one that I would never commit. I would invite the teacher to appear the next day in my office, together with the school principal, with the teaching coordinator, and with someone else responsible for the permanent training of the teachers. In my conversation with the teacher I would ask him or her to prove that this behavior was appropriate, pedagogically, scientifically, humanly, and politically. If it couldn't be proven, which would be the greater likelihood, I would then make an appeal, first hearing the principal's opinion about the teacher who erred, with the understanding that this mistake should not be repeated."

"Very well. But if they should repeat the same process?" asked the young man.

"In that case, I would ask the judicial council of the secretary's office to study the legal means of punishing the teacher. I would rigorously apply the law," I answered.

The entire group understood, and I saw that these young people did not want an undisciplined climate but that they radically refused an arbitrary decision. They wanted a democratic relationship, one of mutual respect. They refused to submit with the blind obedience demanded by the limitless power of the authoritarian; they rejected the irresponsibility of permissiveness.

Perhaps some of them have since taken to the streets, with painted faces, shouting that it was worthwhile to dream.

The next day, with the other group, a restless young woman made the well-articulated comment: "I wanted a school, Paulo, that wasn't like my mother. A school that believed more in young people and that didn't think that some of them are just waiting around to make trouble for others."

Four hours, with ninety adolescents who reinforced in me the joy of living and the right to dream.

NOTES

1. "Teaching Literacy as an Element in the Preparation for Citizenship." Paper read at a meeting sponsored by UNESCO and by the Ministry of Education, Brasilia, 1987.

2. On this point, see Paulo Freire, *Pedagogy of Hope: A Return to the Pedagogy of the Oppressed* (Rio de Janeiro: Paz e Terra, 1992).

3. On this point, see Paulo Freire, *Pedagogy of the Oppressed* (Rio de Janeiro: Paz e Terra, 1970).

From Talking to Learners to Talking to Them and with Them; From Listening to Learners to Being Heard by Them

Let us use as a point of departure the attempt to understand the title of this letter, whose first part says: "From talking to learners to talking to them and with them." We could rephrase this first part, without affecting the meaning, like this: "From the moment in which we talk to learners to the moment we talk with them," or "From the need to talk to learners to the need to talk with them," or "It's important to live the balanced, harmonious experience, between talking to learners and talking with them." That is, there are moments in which the teacher, as the authority, talks to the learners, says what must be done, establishes limits without which the very freedom of learners is lost in lawlessness, but these moments, in accordance with the political options of the educator, are alternated with others in which the educator speaks with the learner.

It doesn't hurt to repeat here the statement, still rejected by many people in spite of its obviousness, that education is a political act. Its nonneutrality demands from educators that they take it on as a political act and that they consistently live their progressive and democratic or authoritarian and reactionary past or also their spontaneous, uncritical choice, that they define themselves by being democratic or authoritarian. Permissiveness, which at times gives the impression of leaning toward freedom, ends up working against it. The climate of lawlessness, of free-for-all, that it creates reinforces the authoritarian position. On the other hand, certainly, permissiveness denies the training of the democrat, of men and women freeing themselves in and by fighting for the democratic ideal, just as it denies the "training" of the obedient, of those who have adapted, those of whom the authoritarian dreams. Permissive people are amphibious—they live in the water and on land—they are not complete; they are defined consistently neither by freedom nor by authority.

Their climate is that of a lack of discipline in which their fear is hardened to freedom. So I have spoken of the necessity that they overcome their political indecisiveness and finally define themselves either in favor of freedom, living it authentically, or against it.

As we can see in our analysis, this problem brings up the question of freedom and of authority, of their contradictory relationship, and this is a question we understand much more poorly than lucidly.

The very fact that we are a markedly authoritarian society, with a strong tradition of command rooted in our history, and undeniably inexperienced in democracy, can explain our ambivalence toward freedom and authority.

It is also important to note that this authoritarian ideology of command, which permeates our culture, cuts across the social classes. The authoritarianism of the minister, of the president, of the general, of the school principal, or of the university professor is the same as the authoritarianism of the worker, of the lieutenant or the sergeant, or of the doorman of the building. Any ten centimeters of power between us easily becomes a thousand meters of power and of arbitrary judgment.

But, precisely because we still are not capable, in social practice, of resolving this problem, of having it clear before us, we tend to confuse a certain use of authority with authoritarianism; and likewise, because we deny this, we fall into a lack of discipline or permissiveness, thinking, however, that we are respecting freedom and thus creating democracy. At other times we are really authoritarian, but we believe and proclaim ourselves to be progressive.

In fact, however, just because I reject authoritarianism does not mean I can fall into a lack of discipline, nor that, rejecting lawlessness, I can dedicate myself to authoritarianism. As I once affirmed: One is not the opposite of the other. The opposite, of either manipulative authoritarianism or lawless permissiveness, is democratic radicalism.

I believe these considerations clarify the theme of this letter. I can affirm that if teachers are consistently authoritarian, then they are always the initiators of talk, while the students are continually subjected to their discourse. They speak to, for, and about the learners. They talk from top to bottom, certain of their correctness and of the truth of what they say. And even when they talk with the learners, it is as if they were doing them a favor, underlining the importance and power of their own voices. This is not the way that democratic educators speak with learners, not even when speaking to them. Authoritarian educators are preoccupied with evaluating the students, with seeing whether they are following or not. The training of the learners, though they are critical subjects who should constantly fight for freedom, never moves authoritarian educators. If the educators are permissive, taking the position of "leave it as it is to see what happens," they abandon the learners to themselves and end up speaking neither to nor with the learners.

If, however, educators choose to be democratic and if the distance between their discourse and their practice becomes ever smaller, then in their scholarly daily lives, which they constantly subject to critical analysis, they live the difficult but possible and pleasurable experience of speaking to and with learners. They know that dialogue centered not only on the content to be taught but on life itself, if it is true, not only is valid from the point of view of the act of teaching but also prepares an open and free climate in the ambience of their classroom.

Speaking to and with the learners is an unpretentious but very positive way for democratic teachers to contribute in their school to the training of responsible and critical citizens, which we need so badly and which is indispensable to the development of our democracy. The democratic school, progressively postmodern and not postmodernly traditional and reactionary, has a great role to play in present-day Brazil.

Far be it from me, nevertheless, to insist on the curriculum of the postmodernly progressive school, to think that the "salvation" of Brazil lies in it. Naturally, the viability of the country does not rest solely in the democratic school's preparing critical and capable citizens, but Brazil's salvation will happen because of the democratic school; it needs the democratic school, it won't be accomplished without the democratic school. And it is in the school that the teachers who talk to and with learners, who hear learners, no matter of what tender age they may be, are thus heard by them. It is through hearing the learners, a task unacceptable to authoritarian educators, that democratic teachers increasingly prepare themselves to be heard by learners. But by listening to and so learning to talk with learners, democratic teachers teach the learners to listen to them as well.

The considerations I mentioned above with reference to the authoritarian position and the permissive position can be applied, obviously, to the problem of hearing learners and of being heard by them. This question is crucial to educators' and learners' right to a voice. No one lives democracy fully, nor do they help it to grow, if, first of all, they are interrupted in their right to speak, to have a voice, to say their critical discourse, or, second, if they are not engaged, in one form or another, in the fight to defend this right, which, after all, is also the right to act.

Thus, however, just as learners' freedom in the class needs limits so that it does not lose itself in indiscipline, so the voice of the educator and of the learners needs ethical limits so that it doesn't slip toward the absurd. It is just as immoral to have our voices silenced, our "body interrupted," as to use the voice to falsify the truth, to lie, deceive, deform.

My right to a voice cannot be a limitless right to say what I might understand of the world and of others; my right to a voice cannot be the right to an irresponsible voice that tells lies without any regrets, since one expects from the lie a result favorable to the desires and plans of the liar.

It is necessary and even urgent that the school become a space to gather and engender certain democratic dispositions, such as the disposition to listen to others—not as a favor but as a duty—and to respect them; a disposition toward tolerance, toward deference to the decisions made by the majority that nevertheless does not deny to anyone who differs in opinion the right to express his or her disagreement; the disposition to question, criticize, and debate; the disposition to respect the public matter that among us comes to be treated as a private matter but that as a private matter is not valued.

The extent and depth of the waste among us are incredible. One needs only to read the daily paper or to watch the television news broadcasts to be aware of the two million very expensive pieces of hospital equipment that are thrown away for lack of use because, due to shoddiness of their construction, they deteriorate before their time. Millions of pieces of work almost mysteriously evaporate, leaving behind only traces. If the administrators responsible for such disasters were punished, if they had to either pay the nation or go to jail, obviously with the right to a defense, the situation would improve.

An activity to be included in the normal political-pedagogical life of the school could be the discussion, from time to time, of cases like these. One could discuss with students what such shamelessness represents for us, over both the long and short terms, from the point of view of both the material effects on the economy of embezzlement and the ethical damage that these disasters cause all of us. We must show the statistics to the children, to the young people, and tell them clearly and firmly that the fact that those responsible act indecently does not authorize us, in the intimacy of our school, to damage the tables, destroy the chalk, waste the food, or dirty the walls.

We should not say: "The powerful do it, so why don't I do it? The powerful rob, why shouldn't I do it? The powerful lie, so why can't I?" It is most definitely not right.

No one constructs a serious democracy, which implies radically changing the societal structures, reorienting the politics of production and development, reinventing power, doing justice to everyone, and abolishing the unjust and immoral gains of the all-powerful, without previously and simultaneously working for these democratic preferences and these ethical demands.

One of the mistakes of the mechanistic Marxists was to live without thinking or affirming that because it is part of society's superstructure, education has no role to play before the society is radically transformed in its infrastructure, in its material conditions. Before such a transformation, what can be done is the dissemination of ideological propaganda for the mobilization and organization of the masses. In this, as in everything else, the mechanists failed. Worse yet, they delayed the struggle in favor of a socialism that they opposed to democracy.[1]

Another democratic disposition, whose opposite is found buried in our authoritarian cultural traditions, is the disposition to respect others; another is tolerance, from which racism and machismo flee like a devil from the cross.

The exercise of this democratic disposition in a truly open school or in one that is opening up must first approach the authoritarian tendency, racist or machista, itself, such as the denial of democracy, of freedoms, and of the rights of those who are different, as the denial of a necessary humanism. Second, the antidemocratic tendency, no matter which one it may be, must be approached as an expression of all this and yet as an incomprehensible contradiction when it is expressed in the practice of men or women recognized as progressive.

What can be said, for example, of a man considered to be progressive who, in spite of his talk in favor of the lower classes, behaves like the lord of his family, whose domineering suffocates his wife and children?

What can be said of the woman who fights for the interests of those of her gender but who at home rarely thanks the cook for the cup of water that she brings her and who, in conversations with friends, refers to the cook as one of "those people"?

It is truly difficult to make a democracy. Democracy, like any dream, is not made with spiritual words but with reflection and practice. It is not what I say that says I am a democrat, that I am not racist or machista, but what I do. What I say must not be contradicted by what I do. It is what I do that bespeaks my faithfulness or not to what I say.

In the struggle between saying and doing in which we must engage to diminish the distance between them, it is just as possible to change what is said to make it fit the doing as it is to change the doing to make it fit what is said. This is why consistency ends up forcing a new choice. In the moment when I discover the inconsistency between what I say and what I do—progressive discourse, authoritarian practice—if, reflecting, at times painfully, I learn the ambiguity in which I find myself, I feel I am not able to continue like this and I look for a way out. In this way, a new choice is imposed on me. Either I change the progressivist discourse for a discourse consistent with my reactionary practice, or I change my practice for a democratic one, adapting it to the progressivist discourse. Finally, there is a third option: the option to assume cynicism, which consists of opportunistically incarnating inconsistency.

I think that one of the ways of helping democracy among us is to combat clearly and with assurance the innocent arguments that are founded on reality or on a partial reality, such as that it is not worthwhile to vote; that politics are always like this, generally impudent and shameful; that all politicians are the same: "For this reason, I am now going to vote for those who do things, even if they steal."

In truth, things are different. This is the way that it is becoming possible for us to engage in politics, but this is not necessarily the way that we always have to do politics. It is not politics that make us like this. We are the ones that engage in these kinds of politics, and indisputably the politics that we engage in now are better than those of my childhood. And, finally, not all the politicians that behave this way are in the different levels of government and in different political parties.

As educators we cannot excuse ourselves from responsibility in the fundamental question of Brazilian democracy and of how to participate in the search for its perfection.

As educators we are politicians; we engage in politics when we educate. And if we dream about democracy, let us fight, day and night, for a school in which we talk to and with the learners so that, hearing them, we can be heard by them as well.

NOTES

1. See Paulo Freire, *Pedagogy of Hope: A Return to the Pedagogy of the Oppressed* (Rio de Janeiro: Paz e Terra, 1992).

EIGHTH LETTER

Cultural Identity and Education

We need to ask ourselves about the relationship between cultural identity, which always cuts across social classes, the subjects of education, and educational practice. The identity of the subjects has to do with the fundamental issues of the curriculum, as much with what is hidden as what is explicit and, obviously, with questions of teaching and learning.

Therefore, it seems to me that before we can begin to discuss the question of the identity of the subjects of education, that is, educators and learners, we must point out that "cultural identity," an expression that we use more and more, cannot pretend to exhaust the whole meaning of the phenomenon "identity." The attribute "cultural," expanded from the restrictive attribute "class," does not exhaust the understanding of the term "identity." In reality, we men and women become special and singular beings. We have been able, through a long human history, to distinguish ourselves, by our own decisions, as individuals among the whole of humanity, but still within the workings of society, without which we also would not be what we are. In truth, we are neither only what we inherit nor only what we acquire but, instead, stem from the dynamic relationship between what we inherit and what we acquire.

There is something in what we inherit and in what François Jacob[1] emphasizes in an interview with *Le Courrier L'UNESCO* that is of the highest importance for the understanding of our topic. "We are programmed, but to learn," says Jacob. And it is exactly because it was possible for us, with the invention of human existence—something more than life itself and that we created with the materials that life offered us—to distinguish ourselves as individuals, to determine what we are and will be. But furthermore, it is with the social invention of language, with which we talk about the world, that we extend the natural world, which we didn't make, into the cultural and historical worlds, which are our products, and that we become animals who are permanently inscribed in a process of learning and seeking, a process that is only made possible, to quote Jacob again, as long as "we can't live unless for tomorrow."

Learning and seeking—to which necessarily are joined teaching and knowing, which in turn can't ignore freedom, which is not a gift but is, rather, something indispensable and necessary, a sine qua non for which we must fight incessantly—make up part of our way of being in the world. And it is exactly because we are programmed but not predetermined, because we are conditioned but, at the same time, conscious of the conditioning, that we become fit to fight for freedom as a process and not as an endpoint. It is for this reason too that the fact that, as Jacob says, "all beings contain in their chromosomes all of their own future" does not in any way mean that our freedom is smothered, is submerged in hereditary structures as if the possibility of our living this freedom disappeared in such structures.

Conditioned, programmed, but not predetermined, in the cultural frame we take advantage of a minimum of freedom to amplify that freedom. In this way, as Jacob points out, through education also as a cultural expression, we can "explore, more or less, the possibilities inscribed in the chromosomes."[2]

The importance of the identity of each one of us as an agent, educator or learner, of the educational practice is clear, as is the importance of our identity as a product of a tension-filled relationship between what we inherit and what we acquire. At times in this relationship, what we acquire ideologically in our social and cultural experiences of class interferes vigorously in the hereditary structures through the power of interests, of emotions, feelings, and desires, of what one usually calls "the strength of the heart." Thus we are not only one thing or another, neither solely what is innate nor solely what is acquired.

The so-called strength of the blood, to use a popular expression, exists, but it is not a determining factor. Just as the presence of the cultural factor, alone, does not explain everything.

In truth, freedom, like a creative deed of human beings, like an adventure, like an experience of risk and of creation, has a lot to do with the relationship between what we inherit and what we acquire.

The impediments to our freedom are much more the products of social, political, economic, cultural, historical, and ideological structures than of hereditary structures. We cannot doubt the power of cultural inheritance, cannot doubt that it makes us conform and gets in the way of our being. But the fact that we are programmed beings, conditioned and conscious of the conditioning and not predetermined, is what makes it possible to overcome the strength of cultural inheritance. The transformation of the material world, of material structures to which a critical-educational effort is joined simultaneously, is the way to overcoming, never mechanically, this inheritance.

What is not possible, nevertheless, in this effort to overcome certain cultural inheritances that repeat themselves from generation to generation and at times seem to be petrified, is to cease to take their existence into consideration. It is very true that the infrastructural changes sometimes very quickly alter ways of being and thinking that have lasted for a long time. On the other hand, to recognize the existence of cultural inheritances should imply respect for them. Such respect does not in any way mean our adaptation to them. Our recognition of them and our respect for them are fundamental conditions for the efforts for change. On the other hand, it is necessary for us to be clear about an obvious fact: These cultural inheritances undeniably cut across social classes. It is in these cultural inheritances that much of our identity is constituted and is thus marked by the social class to which we belong.

Let's think a little about the learners' cultural identity and about the respect that we owe it in our educational practice.

I believe that the first step toward this respect is the recognition of our identity, the recognition of what we are in the practical activity in which we engage. It is by doing things in a certain way, by thinking or speaking in a certain way (for example, saying *canáoes de que mais gosto* 'the songs [of] which I most like' and not *canáoes que mais gosto* 'the songs that I most like', without the preposition *de* 'of' governing the pronoun *que*), by having certain likes and habits that I recognize myself in a certain way, as being similar to other people like me. These other people have a class categorization identical or similar to mine. It is in experiencing the differences that we discover ourselves as I's and you's. Precisely, it is always you as an other who constitutes me as an I as long as I, like the you of the other person, constitute that person as an I.

We have a strong tendency to affirm that what is different from us is inferior. We start from the belief that our way of being is not only good but better than that of others who are different from us. This is intolerance. It is the irresistible preference to reject differences.

The dominant class, then, because it has the power to distinguish itself from the dominated class, first, rejects the differences between them but, second, does not pretend to be equal to those who are different; third, it does not intend that those who are different shall be equal. What it wants is to maintain the differences and keep its distance and to recognize and emphasize in practice the inferiority of those who are dominated.

One of the challenges to progressive educators, in keeping with their choice, is not to feel or to proceed as if they were inferior to dominant-class learners in the private schools who arrogantly mistreat and belittle middle-class teachers. But on the other hand, nor should they feel superior, in the public school system, to the learners from the slums, to the lower-class children, to the children with no comforts, who do not eat well, who do not "dress nicely," who do not "speak correctly," who speak with their own syntax, semantics, and accent.

What falls to the progressive, coherent educators in the two cases is not, in the first, to assume an aggressive position of simply taking revenge or, in the second, to let themselves be tempted by the hypothesis that these children, these poor little ones, are naturally incapable. In the first case, educators must take neither a position of revenge nor of submission but the position of one who assumes responsible authority as an educator; nor, in the second case, may educators take a paternalistic or scornful attitude toward the lower-class children.

The point of departure for this comprehensive practice is knowing, is being convinced, that education is a political practice. Let's repeat, then, that the educator is a politician. In consequence, it is absolutely necessary that educators act in a way consistent with their choice—which is political—and furthermore that educators be ever more scientifically competent, which teaches them how important it is to know the concrete world in which their students live, the culture in which their students' language, syntax, semantics, and accent are found in action, in which certain habits, likes, beliefs, fears, desires are formed that are not necessarily easily accepted in the teachers' own worlds.

In particular, the preparatory teaching work cannot be realized in a context in which one thinks theoretically but at the same time makes a point of staying very far away from and indifferent to the concrete context of the immediate world of action and of sensitivity to the learners.

To think that such work can be realized when the theoretical context is separated in such a way from the learners' concrete experiences is only possible for one who judges that the content is taught without reference to and independently from what the learners already know from their experiences prior to entering school. It is not conceivable for one who rightly rejects the unsustainable division between concrete context and theoretical context.

Content cannot be taught, except in an authoritarian, vanguardist way, as if it was a set of things, pieces of knowledge, that can be superimposed on or juxtaposed to the conscious body of the learners. Teaching, learning, and knowing have nothing to do with this mechanistic practice.

Educators need to know what happens in the world of the children with whom they work. They need to know the universe of their dreams, the language with which they skillfully defend themselves from the aggressiveness of their world, what they know independently of the school, and how they know it.

Two or three years ago, two professors from the University of Campinas, the physicist Carlos Arguelo and the mathematician Eduardo Sebastiani Ferreira, participated in a university meeting in Parant in which the teaching of mathematics and science in general was discussed. On returning to the hotel, after the first morning of activities, they found a group of children flying a kite in an abandoned field. They approached the children and began to converse with them.

"How many meters of line do you usually let loose to fly the kite?" asked Sebastiani.

"Fifty meters, more or less," said a boy named Gelson.

"How do you figure out that you have let loose more or less than fifty meters of line?" questioned Sebastiani.

"Every so often, at about two meters more or less," said the boy, "I make a knot in the line. As the line is running through my hand, I count the knots and so I know how many meters of line I've released."

"And how high do you think the kite is right now?" asked the mathematician.

"Forty meters," said the boy.

"How do you figure?"

"According to how much line I let out and the bow that the line is making."

"We could figure out that problem based on trigonometry or by its similarity to triangles," said Sebastiani.

The boy, in the meantime, said, "If the kite were high, well over my head, it would be the same number of meters high as of line that I let loose, but since the kite is far from my head, leaning down, it is lower than the loose meters of line."

"There was, then, a calculation of degrees," said Sebastiani.

Next, Arguelo asked the boy about the construction of the reel, and Gelson answered making use of the four fundamental operations. Ironically, finished the physicist, Gelson (as much a person as Gerson, I say) had failed mathematics in school. Nothing of what he knew had any value in school because what he knew he had learned through his experience, in the concreteness of his context. He did not talk about his knowledge in a formal and well-composed language, mechanically memorized, which is the only language the school recognized as legitimate.

A worse thing happens in the area of language, in which the syntax, orthography, semantics, and accent of the kind spoken by lower-class children are almost always denigrated.

I have never said, as is sometimes believed, or even suggested that lower-class children should not learn the so-called educated norm of the Portuguese language of Brazil. What I have said is that the problems of language always involve ideological questions and, along with them, questions of power. For example, if there is an "educated norm," it is because there is another style considered uneducated. Who identified the uneducated one as such? What I have actually said and for which I am beaten is that the educated norm should be taught to lower-class children but that in so doing it should also be stressed that

- their language is as rich and beautiful as the educated norm and that therefore they do not have to be ashamed of the way they talk;
- even so, it is fundamental that they learn the standard syntax and intonation so that
  A. they diminish the disadvantages in their struggle to live their lives;
  B. they gain a fundamental tool for the fight they must wage against the injustice and discrimination targeted at them.

Thinking and acting like this are, I feel, in keeping with my progressive, anti-elitist choice. I am not one of those who opposed Lula for president of the Republic of Brazil because he says *menas verdade [sic]* 'less truth' and voted for Collor with so much less truth.

In conclusion, the democratic school should not only be permanently open to its students' contextual reality in order to understand them better and to exercise its teaching activity better, but it should also be disposed to learn of its relationship with the concrete context. Thus, proclaiming itself democratic, it must be truly humble in order to be able to recognize itself, often learning from one who was never schooled.

The democratic school that we need is not one in which only the teacher teaches, in which only the student learns, and in which the principal is the all-powerful commander.

NOTES

1. François Jacob, "Nous sommes programmé mais pour apprendre," *Courrier de L'UNESCO* (February 1991).

2. Ibid.

NINTH LETTER

Concrete Context/
Theoretical Context

In this letter I am going to take as the focus of my thoughts not only the relationship that the concrete and the theoretical contexts establish between themselves but also the way in which we behave in each one of them.

The idea, or one of the main ideas, that motivates me to deal with this topic is to emphasize the importance of this relationship in all that we do in our day-to-day experience as well as in our social and historical experience. We deal daily with relationships, between things, between objects, between words in the composition of sentences and between these words themselves in the structure of the text; among people, in the way that they bond—the aggressiveness, the lovingness, the indifference, the rejection, the surreptitious or open discrimination; between educators and learners, between thinking subjects and knowable objects. Let me make clear from the start that it is not one of my objectives in this letter to deal with the entire group of relationships that we practice and in which we involve ourselves daily; rather, I intend to deal with those that take place between the concrete context and the theoretical one, in the relationship of one with the other.

I believe that one of the affirmations to be made is that in both the animate and the inanimate world, the fundamental condition of life is the condition of relationship, relationship to oneself and to the surrounding world.

We are, therefore, the only beings capable of being both the objects and the subjects of the relationships that we weave with others and with the history that we make and that makes and remakes us. Between us and the world, relationships can be critically, naively, or magically perceived, but we are aware of these relationships to an extent that does not exist between any other living being and the world.

As soon as we began to know not only that we lived but also that we knew that we lived and that, therefore, we could know more, we who practiced in the world began the process of learning about the practice itself. When we did so, the world gradually stopped being merely a solid support[1] on which we stood; instead, it gradually became the world with which we are in a relationship, and finally, simply moving in the world became practice in the world.

It is thus that the practice slowly became action on the world, developed little by little by subjects becoming conscious of carrying out this practice on the world. It was the practice that founded talk about it and consciousness of it. There would be no practice, there would be mere moving in the world, if by moving in the world a person did not become capable of knowing what he or she was doing, and why, in that movement. It was the consciousness of moving that promoted moving to the category of practice and forced practice to generate the knowledge of itself. In this sense, consciousness of practice implies the science that is built into the practice, that is proclaimed in it. In this way, to do science is to discover, to unveil truths about the world, about living beings, about things, truths that were awaiting the unveiling; it is to give objective meaning to the new needs that, emerging from the social practice, confront women and men.

Science, a human activity that occurs in the history that women and men make with their practice, is not, for this very reason, an a priori of history.

The practice of which we are conscious demands and promotes its own science. Thus we cannot forget the relationship between production, the technique indispensable to it, and science.

"One of the sciences that most benefited from production," says Adolfo Vasquez, "is physics." Its birth as such is very recent: It was not known in its characteristic state in Ancient Greece or in the Middle Ages. The weak development of productive forces in the Greek slave society and under feudalism made it unnecessary to create physics.

The science of physics arose in the modern age with Galileo and corresponded to the practical needs of fledgling industry.[2]

Within the theoretical context, we must distance ourselves from the concrete world in order to perceive how theory is built in the practice exercised in the concrete world, even if at times we do not doubt what we know.

Professor Adao Cardoso, a biologist from the University of Campinas, told me that he was invited by a young Indian man from the interior of the Amazon region to learn to fish with a spear. In response to the provoking question of the scientist, who asked him why he threw the spear not at the fish but between the fish and the side of the boat, the man answered, "No, I threw it at the fish. You didn't see it correctly because sometimes one's eyes lie." The Indian explained in his own way, to the level of the "science" that his practice allowed, the phenomenon of refraction.

Based on his own practice and the practice of his village, the young Indian had intimate knowledge of the phenomenon and worked it wisely. He did not, however, understand the "raison d'être" of the phenomenon.

There is still something more that I would like to comment on in relation to these two contexts and how we behave in them.

Let's begin with the concrete context. Let's think about important moments of one day in our lives.[3] We wake up, take our morning showers, leave home for work. We run into people we know and people we don't know. We obey the traffic lights: If they are green, we cross the streets; if they are red, we stop to wait. We do all this without ever once asking ourselves why we do it. We realize that we do it, but we don't ask the reasons. It is this that characterizes our moving around in the concrete world of daily life. We act in it on the basis of bits of knowledge that, having been learned throughout our socialization, have become automatic habits. And because we act like this, our minds do not function epistemologically. Our curiosity is not "aroused" to search for the reasons that things are as they are. Our minds are capable simply of perceiving that something did not occur as expected or that it was processed differently; of letting us know early, almost instantaneously, that there is something wrong.

Let's go on a little further and see how we move in the concrete context of our work, in which the relationship between practice and knowledge of the practice are inseparable. But even though they are inseparable, in the practical, concrete context we do not always act in an epistemologically curious way. We do things because we are in the habit of doing them. Even though in this situation we are more likely to assume the curiosity typical of one who seeks the reasons for things than we are in the situation from daily life described earlier, we still largely do not do it. The ideal in our permanent training is that we convince ourselves of, and prepare ourselves for, the most systematic use of our epistemological curiosity.

The central question that is posed to us as educators during our permanent training is how, from the theoretical context, distancing ourselves from our practice, do we separate our practice from our knowledge of our practice, from the science that it is based on? In other words, how, from the theoretical context, do we "distance ourselves" from our practice and how do we become epistemologically curious in order to then understand our practice in its reason for being?

It is by exposing what we do to the light of the knowledge that science and philosophy offer that we correct and perfect ourselves. It is this that I call "thinking the practice," and it is by thinking the practice that I learn to think and to practice better. And the more I think and act like this, the more I am convinced, for example, that it is impossible to teach content without knowing how students think in the context of their daily lives, without knowing what they know independently of school so that we can, on the one hand, help them to know better what they already know and, on the other, teach them what they don't know yet.

We cannot stop taking into consideration the unfavorable material conditions that many students of schools in marginalized areas of the city experience: the precariousness of their living quarters, the deficiency of their food, the lack of reading activities in their daily lives and of study in their schools, the violence and death that they know almost intimately. In general, none of this is given much consideration, either in basic schooling, from the first grade, in which these children study, or in the teacher training schools. All of this, nevertheless, has an enormous role in the lives of the Carloses, the Marias, the Carmens. All this undeniably affects the cultural being of these children.

Once I was sought out—as happens from time to time—by a group of young women who were finishing the teacher training course in a school in São Paulo.

They were middle-class young women, with good living conditions. They said they were frightened, almost as if they were being threatened, in the face of the possibility that sooner or later they would take over some class in a school in the poor areas.

"We finished the entire degree without anyone ever telling us what a slum is or what slum children are like. What we know of these areas of the city, through television and the newspapers, is that they are an arena of absolute violence and that the children become criminals quickly," they said.

The young women spoke to me of the slum as if it had created itself rather than being a result of the struggle for survival to which the unjust structures of a perverse society push those who have been "displaced from life." They talked to me of the slum as if it were the refuge of ethical deviation and a place for lost souls. And they talked to me of the slum children almost without hope.

In the face of all this, I, at least, do not see any other way to go with my legitimate anger, with my just ire, with my necessary indignation than the political-democratic struggle from which the indispensable transformation in the Brazilian society can result and without which the existing state of affairs worsens rather than disappearing.

Thus, great works for me are not the huge tunnels crossing the city from one neighborhood to another or the parks full of greenery in the nice areas of the city. They are all part of great work also; however, priority must go to working for the humanization of the life of those who have been prohibited from living decently since the "invention" of Brazil: the lower classes.

In the theoretical context, that of the continuing training of educators, critical reflection on our conditioning by our cultural context, on our way of acting, and on our values is indispensable. We must reflect on the influence that our economic difficulties exert over us, on how they can get in the way of our capacity to learn, even though they lack the power to "stupidify" us. The theoretical, preparatory context can never be transformed into a context of pure doing, as is sometimes believed. It is, on the contrary, the context of tasks, of praxis, that is, of practice and of theory.

The dialectic between practice and theory should be fully lived in the theoretical contexts of the training of groups of educators. The idea that it is possible to train educators practically, teaching them to say "Good morning" to their students, teaching them how to shape the hand of the learner in tracing a line, without any serious living with the theory, is as scientifically wrong as is the idea of making speeches, of giving theoretical lessons, without taking into consideration concrete reality, be it that of teachers or that of teachers and their students. That is, such attempts fail to respect the context of the practice that explains how one practices, that is, how one leads to knowing the practice itself; such attempts fail to recognize that theoretical discourse, no matter how correct it might be, cannot superimpose itself on the knowledge generated in the practice of another context.

All this implies a distorted understanding of the practice itself, of the theory. The prepackaged teaching materials to which I have referred earlier in "First Words" are an excellent example of this distorted understanding of the practice and of the theory, an excellent example of how even progressives can act in a reactionary way.

Forty years ago, when I was the director of Education of Social Service of the Industry (SESI) of Pernambuco,[4] one of the battles in which I became embroiled was that of confronting the insistence with which working-class parents demanded that their children learn to read and write beginning with the ABCs, with the alphabet, with the letters rather than the sentences that implied words in relation to each other and in the structure of thought.

"It was like this, with the chart of the ABCs in hand, memorizing the letters that everyone that I know and who knows how to read, learned. My grandfather learned like this. My father learned like this. I did, too. Why not my child?" they said almost in unison in the so-called circles of parents and teachers that I coordinated. It was by participating in those meetings, those debates, that I became aware, on the one hand, that the social practice in which we take part generates a corresponding knowledge of itself and that, on the other hand, the complete "knowledge of experience" has to be respected. Even more, conquering this awareness happens through knowledge.

I remember, even today, how I gradually learned to be consistent and that consistence is not conniving. On the one hand, by that time I was already defending families' right to participate in the debate about the school's educational policy itself, but, on the other hand, I recognized the great mistakes of the parents, such as, for example, their demand that we teach their children to be literate beginning with the letters or their constant requests to be harsh with the children. Many of the parents said: "Spanking is what makes a man macho. Punishment is what teaches the child to learn."

These ideas, or some of them, were shared at times by teachers who, in their deepest selves, "housed" the dominant authoritarian ideology. In truth, just as much (or almost) as were the parents, some of the teachers were afraid of and angry at freedom, afraid of the learners, and closed themselves off not only from perceiving how many demands there were in the process of knowing but also from the passions and the rewards of being instigators of happiness.

My voyage through SESI was a time of profound learning. I learned, for example, that my coherence would not be, on the one hand, in giving in to the parents who demanded of us the mistakes referred to earlier nor, on the other hand, in silencing them at least with the power of our discourse. On the one hand, we could not reject them by resoundingly saying "no" to everything, affirming that it was not scientific, nor could we accept everything in an attempt to give an example of democratic respect. We couldn't be lukewarm. We needed to support their initiatives since we had invited them and told them that they had the right to give opinions, to criticize, to suggest. But, on the other hand, we could not say "yes" to everything. The answer was political-pedagogical: It was the debate, the frank conversation in which we tried to clarify our position in the face of their pleas.

Even now I remember the frightened, surprised, interested, or curious faces of the overwhelming majority of mothers and fathers of all the schools that we maintained when, during sessions of our circles of parents and teachers, I asked them to tell me if they knew of any child who had begun to speak by saying "FLM."

After a silence, interrupted by indecisive smiles, after some movement of elbows, lightly nudging the arm of a neighbor as if they were saying "Go on!," one of them, with the approval of the rest, would say, "I, at least, saw many children begin to speak, but I never saw any of them begin by saying letters. It was always by saying 'Mommy,' 'bread,' 'no,' 'I want.'"

Therefore I would like for us to think about the following: Women and men, when they were children, began to speak by saying not letters but words that meant sentences—when the baby cries and says "Mama," the child probably means: "Mommy, I'm hungry" or "Mommy, I'm wet." These words with which babies begin to talk are called "one-word sentences," that is, sentences of or with only one word. Thus, if all of us begin to speak like this, how, then, in the moment of learning to write and read, should we begin by memorizing letters?

No one rigorously teaches anyone to speak. People learn in the world, in their homes, in society, in the street, in the neighborhood, in school. Speech, the language of people, is an acquisition. People acquire speech socially. Speech comes much before writing, just as a certain "writing," or the announcement of it, comes much before what people call writing. And just as it is necessary to speak in order to speak, it is necessary to write in order to write. No one writes if they don't write, just as no one learns to walk if not by walking.

For this very reason, we should stimulate children as much as possible to speak and write. It is their scribbling, unarguably a form of writing, that we should praise and that is a beginning of writing to be stimulated. We should praise the fact that they write, that they tell their stories, that they invent and reinvent the popular tales of their environment.

It was in conversations more or less like this that we were transforming the circles of parents and teachers into a theoretical context in which we searched for the reasons that things are as they are.

I remember one conversation in particular that I had with an anguished mother. She told me of her ten-year-old child, whom she considered "impossible," "angry," "disobedient," "diabolical," "unbearable." "The only thing I can do is to tie him to a tree trunk in the garden," she concluded with a face as if she were at that moment tying up the child.

I said, "Why don't you change the means of punishment a little? Look, I'm not saying that you should do away with punishment altogether. Even little Peter would think it was strange if, as of tomorrow, you did nothing more to punish him. I am only saying that you should change the punishment. Choose some way of making him feel that you reject a certain behavior of his. But through a less violent means. On the other hand, you need to show little Peter, first of all, that you love him, second, that he has rights and duties. He has the right, for example, to play, but he has the duty to respect others; the right to find study boring and tiresome, but also the duty to fulfill his obligations. Peter, like all of us, needs limits.

No one can do what they want. Without limits social life would be impossible.

"But it is not by tying little Peter up or daily haranguing him about his 'mistakes' that you are going to help your son to be better. Thus it is necessary to change little by little the way of being or of gradually being part of his own home. It is necessary to change the relationship with Peter gradually so that his life can change as well. It is necessary to overcome the difficulty of conversing with him."

Little Peter's father had left home a year ago. The mother worked very hard washing clothes for two or three families and was helped by a younger sister. When we said good-bye, she squeezed my hand. She seemed hopeful.

A month later, she was in the first row of the classroom in the meeting of parents and teachers. In the middle of the meeting, she stood up to defend the moderation of punishment, greater tolerance by the parents, a friendlier interaction between them and their children, even though she recognized how difficult this so often was, considering the real difficulties of their lives.

On the way out, she squeezed my hand and said, "Thank you. I no longer use that tree trunk." She smiled, sure of herself, and went off with the other mothers who were also leaving the school.

As a practical-theoretical context, the school cannot ignore knowledge about what happens in the concrete contexts of its students and their families. How can we understand students' difficulties during the process of becoming literate without knowing what happens in their experiences at home or how much contact they have with written words in their sociocultural context?

The child who is a daughter of intellectuals, who sees her parents working with reading and writing, is one case; the child of parents who don't read and, furthermore, who do not see more than five or six flashes of electoral propaganda and the occasional commercial advertisements is another.

When I was municipal secretary of education in the government of Luíza Erundina (1989–1991), in one of the many interviews that I gave I raised the question of the possibility that some business, with the pedagogical orientation of the Secretariat, might accept the project of "planting sentences" in important places of neighborhoods where many illiterate people reside. The intent was to provoke the curiosity of the children and the adults. These would be sentences that had to do with the social practice of the area and that were not foreign to it; sentences that would also be approved by the schools around the region of the experience.

When I lived and worked in Chile as an exile, in an agrarian reform zone in which the work of adult literacy was developed, I happily with surprise saw sentences and words engraved on the tree trunks by those becoming literate. The sociologist Maria Edi Ferreira has called those farmers "sowers of words."[5]

I don't want anyone to think that a community that is illiterate today can become literate tomorrow only because we "plant words and sentences" in it. No! A community becomes literate insofar as new social needs, material and also spiritual, demand it. It is possible, however, that we can help children read and write using artifices like "planting" sentences before the changes occur.

The continuing training of the learner, which implies the critical reflection on practice, is founded exactly on this dialectic between practice and theory. The training groups, in which this practice of plunging into the practice in order to enlighten what is given as well as the process in which what is given is given are, if well realized, a better way of living, continuous training.[6] The first point to be made about the training groups from the progressive perspective in which I situate myself is that they are not productive without the existence of a democratic, alert, curious, humble, and scientifically competent leadership. Without these qualities, the training groups are not realized as true theoretical contexts. Without this leadership, whose scientific competence should be greater than that of the groups, one neither unveils the intimacy of the practice, nor can one plunge into it and, enlightening it, perceive the mistakes and the errors committed, the "betrayals" of the ideology, or the obstacles that make the process of knowing difficult.

A second aspect that concerns the working of the groups is what is attached to the knowledge that the groups should have of themselves. This is the problem of their identity, without which they can solidly come together only with great difficulty. And, if they don't gain such knowledge throughout their experiences, it is not possible for them to know clearly what they want or how to go about dealing with what they want, which implies knowing why, against what, in favor of what, and whom they engage in the improvement of their own knowledge.

The practice of thinking and studying the practice takes us to the perception of the previous perception or to the knowledge of the previous knowledge that, generally, involves a new knowledge.

As long as we go forth in the theoretical context of the training groups, in the illumination of practice and the discovery of misunderstandings and errors, we are also necessarily broadening the horizon of scientific knowledge, without which we do not "arm" ourselves to overcome the errors committed and perceived. This necessary expansion of horizons that is born from the attempt to respond to the need that first made us reflect on practice tends to increase its lens. The clarification of a point here reveals another there that also needs to be unveiled. This is the dynamic of the process of thinking the practice. It is for this reason that thinking the practice teaches one to think better in the same way that it teaches one to practice better.

In this sense, the intellectual work in a theoretical context demands putting into practice the complete act of studying, from which the critical reading of the world cannot be omitted, involving the reading and writing of the word, reading and writing texts in such a way that they are complete—more than this, in such a way that they identify themselves in the theoretical contexts—in such a way that, if they are efficient, in them it is not fitting to say: "I don't know how to write, I don't know how to read."

I would like to continue to underline the importance of reading newspapers and magazines, of establishing connections between the commented-on facts, occurrences, bad governing, and the life of the school and on the importance of the audience of certain TV programs, duly videotaped, of the deliberate making of videotapes, fixing remnants of practices, even of one of the work sessions of the group. No resource that could help reflection on the practice, that could result in its improvement through the production of more knowledge, can or should be put aside.

To avoid the risk that the study groups, while they are theoretical contexts, will suffer from too narrow a focus, it is important to have periodic interdisciplinary meetings joining different groups for the debate of the same topic, seen under different but pertinent lenses.

An interesting practice would be the exchange of videos between different training groups, including videos about the training work of the groups themselves. Group A sends to B a video in which one of their study sessions had been taped and receives from B another with similar material. Both groups would be obliged to tape their reactions to the activities of the other. The experience of reflection would amplify in an extraordinary way.

In Tanzania, in Equatorial Africa, I had an experience of enormous value. A Canadian movie director filmed the discussion between a farming community and an agronomist about the crops of the next agricultural season. Right away, showing the film to another community 100 kilometers away, he filmed the debate about the previous community's debate. He returned later to the first community to which he showed the reactions of the friends that they didn't even know.

In this way, he lessened the distance between the communities, he increased the knowledge about the country, he established necessary ties between them, and he made possible a more critical level of understanding of the national reality.

Within a short time, the film director told me, he covered a great part of Tanzania, which created for him, obviously, certain problems connected with the more backward areas of the country.

To challenge the people to read the world critically is always an uncomfortable practice for those who base their power on the "innocence" of the exploited.

One who evaluates what I do is my practice, but my practice theoretically enlightened.

NOTES

1. See also Paulo Freire, *Pedagogy of the Oppressed* (Rio de Janeiro: Paz e Terra, 1970).

2. Adolfo Sanchez Vasquez, *Filosofia de Praxis*, 2nd ed. (Rio de Janeiro: Paz e Terra, 1977).

3. See on this point Karel Kosik, *Dialectic of the Concrete* (Rio de Janeiro: Paz e Terra, 1976).

4. See on this point note 5 of Ana Maria Freire, in Paulo Freire, *Pedagogy of Hope: A Return to the Pedagogy of the Oppressed* (Rio de Janeiro: Paz e Terra, 1992).

5. See Freire, *Pedagogy of the Oppressed*.

6. The municipal secretary of education worked during the entire term of Mayor Luíza Erundina on the continuing training of their groups of educators, in cooperation with the University of São Paulo, the University of Campinas, and the Pontiff Catholic University of São Paulo, through training groups to which Professor Madalena Freire Weffort added her original contribution.

Once More the Question of Discipline

I have already referred to the need for learners to develop intellectual discipline in themselves, with the collaboration of the educator. Without discipline, one does not create intellectual work, read texts seriously, write carefully, observe and analyze facts, or establish relationships among them. And may all this not lack the love for adventure, for daring, but neither may it lack a sense of limits so that the adventure and daring to create do not become undisciplined irresponsibility. We must avoid the idea that different and separate disciplines exist, one, the intellectual; another, the discipline of the body, which has to do with schedules and training; still another, the ethical-religious discipline; and so on. It may be that certain objectives require different disciplinary paths. The fundamental one, however, is that, if the required discipline is healthy, if the understanding of the discipline is healthy, if the way of creating it and living it is democratic, if the inventive subjects of the indispensable discipline are healthy, it always implies the experience of limitations, the contradictory play between authority and freedom, and never ignores a solid ethical base. In this sense, I could never understand how, in no ethics' name, an authority can impose an absurd discipline simply to have the freedom to exert the experience of a castrating obedience, accommodating itself to its capacity to be loyal.

There is no discipline in immobility, in indifferent, distant authority that immobilizes freedom, in the authority that dismisses itself in the name of respect for freedom.

But, too, there is no discipline in the immobilization of freedom, on which the authority imposes its will, its preferences, as being the best for freedom, an immobilization to which intimidated freedom or movement of pure revolt is submitted. Discipline can only be found, on the contrary, in the tension between the necessary coercibility of authority and the intense search for the freedom to assume it. For this reason the authority that grows excessively in authoritarianism or atrophies in indiscipline, losing the sense of movement, becomes lost and threatens freedom. In this excessive growth of authority, its movement becomes so robust that it totally immobilizes or distorts the movement of freedom. The freedom immobilized by a violent or extortionist authority is the freedom that, not having been assumed, gets lost in the falsity of inauthentic movements.

For there to be discipline, not only must freedom have the right to say "no" to that which is proposed to it as the truth and the right thing, but it also must exercise that right. Freedom needs to learn to affirm denying, not only by denying but as a criterion of certainty. It is in this movement of coming and going that freedom ends by internalizing authority and becomes a freedom with authority only as, while an authority, it respects freedom.

Our political, social, pedagogical, ethical, aesthetic, and scientific responsibility, as social and historical beings, as bearers of a subjectivity that plays an important role in history, in the process of this contradictory movement between authority and freedom, is of unarguable importance. But in recognizing political responsibility, let's overcome petty politics. In underscoring social responsibility, let's say "no" to the purely individualistic interests. In recognizing pedagogical duties, let's leave aside the pedagogue's illusions. In demanding ethics, let's flee from the ugliness of puritanism and let's dedicate ourselves to the invention of the beauty of purity. Finally, in accepting scientific responsibility, let's reject the distortions of scientism.

Perhaps some reader more "existentially tired" and "historically anesthetized"[1] may say that I am dreaming too much. Dreaming, yes, because as a historical being, if I don't dream I cannot become a being. Too much, no. I even think that we dream these dreams, so fundamentally indispensable to life or the solidification of our democracy, too little. To realize these dreams requires discipline in the act of reading, of writing, or writing and reading, of teaching and learning; in a process that is pleasurable but difficult to learn; discipline in respect and in dealing with public matters; discipline in mutual respect.

To say that as a teacher "the grade in which I teach does not matter; what I may or may not do will have little importance in view of the fact that the powerful act to benefit themselves and against the national interests" is not a worthy statement. It is not an ethical affirmation. It is simply self-indulgent and accommodating. Worse, if accommodated, my immobility becomes a motor to drive more shamelessness. My immobility, whether or not it is produced by fatalistic motives, acts effectively in favor of the injustices that are perpetuated or the catastrophes that afflict us, in favor of delaying urgent solutions.

No one receives democracy as a gift. One fights for democracy. The bonds that prohibit us from being democratic are broken not by a well-behaved patience but by the people mobilizing, organizing, being consciously critical; by the lower class-majorities not only feeling that they have been exploited since Brazil was invented but also joining together on feeling the knowledge that they are being exploited, the knowledge that gives them the "reason for being" of the phenomenon that they reach largely at the level of sensitivity to it.

When I speak of sensitivity to the phenomenon and of critical apprehension of the phenomenon, I am in no way suggesting any division between sensitivity, emotions, and cognitive activity. I already said that I know with my whole self: feelings, emotions, and critical mind.

Let's make clear that people mobilizing, people organizing, people knowing in critical terms, people deepening and solidifying democracy against any authoritarian adventure are also people forging the necessary discipline, a discipline without which democracy does not function. In Brazil, we almost always go back and forth between the absence of discipline by the denial of liberty and the absence of discipline by the absence of authority.

We lack discipline at home, in school, on the streets, in traffic. The number of those who die on the weekends through pure lack of discipline, what the country wastes in these accidents, in the ecological disasters, is astonishing.

Another lack of apparent respect for others, as ominous as the way that we were becoming undisciplined, is the lawlessness, the lack of responsibility with which killings go on, unpunished, in this country.

Dominated and exploited in the capitalist system, the lower classes need—at the same time that they engage in the process of forming an intellectual discipline—to create a social, civic, and political discipline, which is absolutely essential to the democracy that goes beyond the pure bourgeois and liberal democracy and that, finally, seeks to conquer the injustice and the irresponsibility of capitalism.

This is one of the tasks to which we must dedicate ourselves rather than to the mere task of teaching, in the erroneous sense of transmitting the knowledge to the learners.

The teacher must teach. It is necessary to do it. But teaching is not transmitting knowledge. For the act of teaching to be constituted as such, the act of learning must be preceded by or concomitant with the act of learning the content or the knowable object, with which the learners also become producers of the knowledge that was taught to them.

Only insofar as learners become thinking subjects, and recognize that they are as much thinking subjects as are the teachers, is it possible for the learners to become productive subjects of the meaning or knowledge of the object. It is in this dialectic movement that teaching and learning become knowing and reknowing. The learners gradually know what they did not yet know, and the educators reknow what they knew before.

This way of not only understanding the process of teaching and of learning but of living it demands the discipline of which I have been speaking, discipline that cannot separate itself from political discipline, essential to the invention of citizenship. Yes, citizenship—above all in a society like ours, of such authoritarian and racially, sexually, and class-based discriminatory traditions—is really an invention, a political production. In this sense, one who suffers any of the discriminations, or all of them at once, does not enjoy the full exercise of citizenship as a peaceful and recognized right. On the contrary, it is a right to be reached and whose conquest makes democracy grow substantively. Citizenship implies freedom—to work, to eat, to dress, to wear shoes, to sleep in a house, to support oneself and one's family, to love, to be angry, to cry, to protest, to support, to move, to participate in this or that religion, this or that party, to educate oneself and one's family, to swim regardless in what ocean of one's country. Citizenship is not obtained by chance: It is a construction that, never finished, demands we fight for it. It demands commitment, political clarity, coherence, decision. For this reason a democratic education cannot be realized apart from an education of and for citizenship.

The more we respect students independently of their color, sex, or social class, the more testimony we will give of respect in our daily lives, in school, in our relationship with colleagues, with doormen, with cooks, with watchmen, with students' mothers and fathers, the more we lessen the distance between what we say and what we do, so much more will we be contributing toward the strengthening of democratic experiences. We will be challenging ourselves, to struggle more in favor of citizenship and its expansion. We will be forging in ourselves the indispensable intellectual discipline without which we impede our training, as well as the no-less-necessary political discipline essential to the struggle for the invention of citizenship.

NOTES

1. For the notions of "existential weariness" and "historical anesthesia" see Paulo Freire, *Pedagogy of Hope: A Return to the Pedagogy of the Oppressed* (Rio de Janeiro: Paz e Terra, 1992).

To Know and to Grow— Everything Yet to See

I close this book with a text, presented in a conference in Recife in April 1992 and in which I clarify some analyses about the concrete context of daily life.

To reflect on the theme implicit in the phrase "to know and to grow—everything yet to see" was the task proposed to me by the organizers of this meeting.

The point of departure of my reflection should be to return to the phrase that is the object of my epistemological curiosity. This entails seeking, first and foremost, to learn the meaning of the phrase, which in turn demands the understanding that the words have in it, in their relationship with each other.

In the first place, we are faced with two blocks of thought: "to know and to grow" and "everything yet to see." The two verbs of the first part, which could be replaced by two nouns, "knowledge" and "growth," are found linked together by the coordinating conjunction "and." In truth, these two blocks hold within themselves the possibility of an opening from which would result the following: The process of knowing and the process of growing have everything to do with each other. Or even: The process of knowing implies that of growing. It is not possible to know without a certain kind of growth. It is not possible to grow without a certain kind of knowledge.

To know is a transitive verb, a verb that expresses an action that, performed by a subject, affects or falls directly on an object without prepositional governing. Thus the complement of this verb may be called a "direct object." One who knows, knows something. "Only I know the pain that hurts me." Pain is the direct object of "I know," the object of my action of knowing.

To grow, on the contrary, is an intransitive verb. It does not need complementation that fixes its meaning. What one can do, and what is almost always done, as a function of the demands of a subject's thinking, with the meaning of verbs like this, is to join to it circumstantial elements or meanings, adverbials. "I grew painfully" or "I grew keeping my curiosity alert" in which "painfully" and "keeping my curiosity alert" express the mode of my process of growing.

Let's focus a little, now, on the process of knowing.

When we ask ourselves about the process of knowing, taken now as a vital phenomenon, we can initially state that, in the first place, it takes place in life and not only in

164

the existence that we, women and men, create throughout history with the materials that life offers us. But it is
the knowledge that we become capable of nurturing that
interests us here rather than a certain type of reaction
that is verified in the relationship that takes place in non-
human life.

As to the question of what knowledge really is, the first
statement to be made is that knowing is a social process,
whose individual dimension, however, cannot be forgot-
ten or even devalued.

The process of knowing, which involves the whole conscious self, feelings, emotions, memory, affects, an epistemologically curious mind, focused on the object, equally
involves other thinking subjects, that is, others also capable of knowing and curious. This simply means that the
relationship called "thinking" is not enclosed in a relationship "thinking subject–knowable object" because it ex-
tends to other thinking subjects.

Another aspect that I think is interesting to emphasize
here is what is said regarding the spontaneous way in
which we move in the world,[1] from which results a certain kind of knowing, of perceiving, of being sensitized by
the world, by objects, by their presence, by the speech of
others. In this spontaneous way in which we move in the
world, we perceive things and facts, we feel ourselves
warned, we behave in one way or another because of
signs whose meaning we internalize. We gain from them
an immediate knowledge, but we don't learn from them

the fundamental reason for being. Our minds, in the spontaneous orientation that we make in the world, do not work epistemologically. They are not directed critically, questioningly, methodically, rigorously, to the world or to the objects to which they are inclined. This is, in the words of Camoes, "knowledge made from experience," which nevertheless lacks the filter of critical thinking. It is innocent wisdom, commonsensical, lacking rigorous methods of approaching the object, but it should not for these reasons be exempt from our consideration. Its necessary conquest happens through our respect for it and has in it its point of departure.

Perhaps it would be interesting to examine one morning of ours as the object of our curiosity and to see the difference between these two ways of our moving in the world, the spontaneous and the systematic ways.

We stir. We wake up. We brush our teeth. We take our first shower of the day, followed by breakfast. We converse with our wives or husbands. We inform ourselves of the first daily news. We leave home. We walk in the street. We bump into people that come and go. We stop at the traffic lights. We wait for the green light, whose meaning we learn in childhood. And at no time do we ask ourselves about any of the things that we did, from brushing our teeth to taking the shower to drinking the coffee (unless we have demanded something outside of the routine) to stopping for the red traffic light. In other words: Immersed in daily life, we go on in it, in its "streets," on its "sidewalks," with no great need to question ourselves about anything. In daily living, our minds do not work epistemologically.

If we proceed a little further in our analysis of the daily life of this morning, in which we analyze ourselves, we can observe that, to have taken any morning of ours as an object of our curiosity, it was necessary to step outside of the experience of daily life. It was necessary for us to emerge from it, then, in order to "distance ourselves" from it, from the way that we move in the world of our mornings. It is interesting to observe, also, that it is in "distancing ourselves" from the object that we "come closer." The "distancing" from the object is epistemologically "coming closer" to it. Only in this way can we "admire" the object, in our case, the morning, in whose time we analyze how we move in the world.

In these two cases I think it is easy to see the substantive difference in position that we occupy, regarding "conscious selves," moving in the world. In the first case, I see myself in agreement with the story that I myself tell about how I move in the morning, and in the second, I perceive myself as the subject that describes his own movements. In the first moment, that of the experience of and in daily living, my conscious self is exposing itself to facts, to deeds, without, nevertheless, asking itself about them, without looking for their "reason for being." I repeat that the knowing—because there also is knowing— that results from these involvements is that made from pure experience. In the second moment, in which our minds work epistemologically, the methodological rigor with which we come closer to the object, having "distanced ourselves" from it, that is, having objectified it, offers us another kind of knowing, a knowing whose exactitude gives to the investigator or the thinking subject a margin of security that does not exist in the first kind of knowing, that of common sense.

This does not mean that we should in any way scorn this innocent knowing, whose necessary conquest comes about through respect for it.

In truth, discussion of these two types of knowing implies a debate over practice and theory that can only be understood if they are perceived and captured in their contradictory relationship. They are never isolated, each one in itself; there is never only theory, never only practice. Thus the sectarian political-ideological positions—positions that, instead of understanding their contradictory relationship exclude one another—are wrong. The anti-intellectualism denies validity to the theory; the theoretical elitism denies validity to the practice. The rigor with which I approach objects prohibits me from leaning toward either of these positions: neither anti-intellectualism nor elitism but practice and theory enlightening each other mutually.

Now let's think a little about "to grow." Let's take "to grow" as an object of our restlessness, of our epistemological curiosity. More than feeling or being touched by the personal and social experience of growing, let's seek the radical meaning of the concept, its ingredients. Let's emerge from daily living, in which we "bump into things," such that we wait for the green light to cross the street, that is, without asking ourselves anything, and let's live the experience of growing. Let's emerge from daily living and, with a curious mind, let's question ourselves about growing.

In our first approach to taking the concept as an object of our knowing, we perceive that it is revealed to us as a vital phenomenon whose experience inserts its subjects in a dynamic movement. Immobility in growth is sickness and death.

Growing plays a part in the experience of life. But precisely because women and men, throughout a long history, end up by becoming capable of taking advantage of the materials that life offers us, creating with them human existence—language, the symbolic world of culture, history—growing in us or among us, "growing" gains a meaning and goes beyond growing in pure life. Growing to us is something more than growing to the trees or the animals that, unlike us, cannot take their own growth as an object of their preoccupation. For us, growing is a process in which we can intervene. The point of decision of human growth is not found in the species. We are indisputably programmed beings, but we are in no way predetermined. And we are programmed above all to learn, as François Jacob points out.[2]

It is our growing to which I refer in this conference paper, not the growing of trees or of the newborn puppies of Andra and Jim, our pair of German shepherds.

It is precisely because we become capable of inventing our existence, something more than the life that it implies but supplants, that growing to us gradually becomes much more complex and problematic, in the rigorous sense of this adjective, than growing is to trees and animals.

As a point of departure for the critical understanding of growing among us, existing, it is important to note that because we are "programmed to learn," we live, or experience, or we find ourselves open to experience the relationship between what we inherit and what we acquire. We become genetic-cultural beings. We are not only nature, nor are we only culture, education, and thinking. Thus growing, to us, is an experience affected by biology, psychology, culture, history, education, politics, aesthetics, and ethics.

It is in growing as a totality that each one of us is, as it is sometimes called in sugary speeches, in the "harmonious growth of being." However, we often lack the disposition of the struggle for the harmonious growth of being, to which we should aspire.

We should aspire to grow normally physically, with the essential organic development; to grow in an emotionally balanced way; to grow intellectually through participation in educational practices quantitatively and qualitatively assured by the government; to grow in good taste before the world; and to grow in mutual respect, toward overcoming all the obstacles that today prohibit the integral growth of millions of human beings spread throughout the different worlds into which the world is divided but, above all, in the Third World.

The statistics of impartial organizations are impressive, organizations like the World Bank and UNICEF which, in their 1990 and 1991 reports, respectively, tell us of the misery, of the levels of infant mortality, of the absence of systematic education, of the alarming number—160 million children—of people who will die in the Third World of measles, of whooping cough, of malnutrition. The UNICEF reports on studies already done to determine the cost of avoiding a total disaster in the present decade: Two-and-a-half billion dollars would be required, the same amount, concluded the report in a somewhat frightened way, that North American industries spend per year to sell more cigarettes.

Knowing has everything to do with growing. But the knowing of dominant minorities absolutely must not prohibit, must not asphyxiate, must not castrate the growing of the immense dominated majorities.

NOTES

1. On this point see Karel Kosik, *Dialectic of the Concrete* (Rio de Janeiro: Paz e Terra, 1976).

2. François Jacob, "Nous sommes programmé mais pour apprendre," *Courrier de L'UNESCO* (February 1991).

Afterword

SHIRLEY STEINBERG

On May 2, 1997, I received an e-mail from Marcia Mores in Brazil. She wrote, "I have sad news. My dear friend Paulo Freire died today." I had not expected to hear this news for many years. Paulo was vibrant, so alive. It was inconceivable to imagine him gone . . . gone from us. A decade later, I now realize that he never left. Paulo's imprint upon our lives is more meaningful, more necessary now, than it was even in the 1970s when he first generated a pedagogy for oppressed and marginalized peoples.

Paulo never intended his work and ideology to be adopted as some sort of gospel, methodology, taxonomy, or educational quick-fix. His early work was specifically designed to apply to those students and teachers with whom he worked and lived. Critics of his work cite his exclusive language, or antienvironmental stance, ignorant of the fact that he originally wrote during a time when there was only one writing discourse, and that was male, and that just because his early writings didn't address the environment, that didn't mean he was not conscious of it. Paulo never wanted to be all things to all people, and those that take issue with his work should, in three words, *not use it*. Ironically, he spent many words during the final years of his life apologizing for unintentional omissions and politically incorrect earlier work. That was Paulo . . . humble, never intending to insert himself into a discourse that would hurt or harm anyone (that is, except for those in the dominant culture).

When it came to those in power, Paulo used his words. He taught that without identifying controlling powers and the hegemonic influences upon citizens, we could never attain empowerment or enlightenment. Our duties, as those who taught the marginalized and disenfranchised, were to facilitate the understanding of the origins and ideologies of those in power, and how this understanding related to oppression. He was fearless in his defense of those without power; he was fearless in his anger and indignation for power-wielding brokers who inserted themselves into our schools and communities.

Paulo didn't have time for defending himself. He was too busy attempting to make pedagogy possible. Those who have spent time asking why they are not empowered by his work or the discourse of critical pedagogy are those who are not able to understand the depth of the commitment and humility that must accompany it. I don't have much hope for them, although I think Paulo never lost hope.

There are those who use Paulo Freire's name and pedagogy to advance their own careers and centers of education. Ignoring Nita Freire's influence and work with Paulo and in his name, arbitrary scholars have used Freire's name to imply that they had a special relationship with Paulo and are heirs to all he said and did. Most of these educational alchemists are in the *Freire Game* for themselves, and with Paulo gone, it is easy to appropriate his work and words. Thankfully, Paulo did not live to see his work bastardized; his beloved wife, Nita, ignored; and his scholarship reduced into pithy conferences, Freirean centers, and, my favorite, yet another *Last Book of Paulo Freire*. A humorous moment occurred in 2005 when a group was organizing a special interest group on Paulo Freire under the auspices of the American Educational Research Association. There were about 150 people in a very hot room in Montreal. César Rossatto chaired the meeting, with humility and love. César asked the twenty or so invited speakers to introduce themselves so around the room we went. The vulgar pomposity many of the speakers used was wonderfully arrogant: *Hello, my name is. . . . I knew Paulo, and he and I. . . . Hi my name is. . . . I was very close to Paulo. He was my best friend. I remember when he and I. . . .* On and on they went. A friend, João Paraskeva, kept me laughing when he suggested that when the circle came around to him he would remark: *Hello, my name is João Paraskeva, and I tied Paulo Freire's shoes.* We all smiled, knowing that Paulo was probably having quite a laugh at the puff coming from the polished scholars of one-upmanship in the room.

Humility is such an important factor in understanding the work and dedication of Paulo Freire. As educators we do not come to the classroom or educational site as the knower of all. We come to share and facilitate that which we are privileged to know. Teaching is an honor and, as Paulo writes in his letters in this book, we are cultural workers who can influence students and open portals of knowledge. But in the end, our students must embrace what they have been offered. We are not indoctrinators, we are teachers—teachers committed to social justice, equity, and humility.

I have been blessed to observe communities that have been able to take the seeds from the pedagogy of Paulo Freire and create conditions that exceed any expectation. The work of the Centre de Recerca Social i Educativa, "Center of Social and Educational Research" (CREA) in Barcelona is one example of the growth from Freire's seeds. Started in the 1970s by Ramón Flecha and his colleague, Jesús Gómez, CREA is an extraordinary example of teachers as cultural workers. Working with the disenfranchised gypsies of Barcelona, the teachers of CREA established literature circles in which small community reading groups taught reading and writing to those who were functionally illiterate. Visiting one such group in 2003, I listened to fifteen participants (most of whom had begun in 1976 or 1977) discuss James Joyce's *Ulysses*.

Speaking in Catalan, the participants quoted Federico García Lorca and other writers as they discussed Joyce and his intentions in writing. Most of the participants had never been formally educated. What miracles happen when a teacher teaches with the mentoring of Paulo Freire.

Another part of Freire's humility dealt with his spirituality. A liberation theologian, Paulo was dedicated to his interpretation of Catholicism and his belief that one could blend both spiritual and social commitment into a way of life. His spirituality reached into the realms of love and his discussions of radical love and commitment permeate his words. There was not a day in Paulo Freire's life where he was not absolutely alive and appreciative of his life and the loves of his life. Paulo knew how lucky he was and did not take any part of his being taken for granted. That is amazing to me, someone who was larger than life, refusing to be anything more than a particle within life, striving only to teach, to serve, and to love.

I sincerely hope that we engage in critical pedagogical work that is respectful and mindful of Paulo Freire, and that we add our own cultural capital and the needs of our own communities to this work.

SUGGESTED READINGS

Darder, A. *Reinventing Paulo Freire: A Pedagogy of Love*. Boulder, CO: Westview Press, 2002.

Freire, A. *Chronicles of Love: My Life with Paulo Freire*. New York: Peter Lang Publishing Group, 2001.

Freire, P., J. Fraser, D. Macedo, T. McKinnon, and W. Stokes, eds. *Mentoring the Mentor: A Critical Dialogue with Paulo Freire*. New York: Peter Lang Publishing Group, 1997.

Kincheloe, J. *Critical Pedagogy Primer*. New York: Peter Lang Publishing Group, 2004.

Macedo, D. *Literacies of Power: What Americans are Not Allowed to Know*. Boulder, CO: Westview Press, 2006.

McLaren, P. *Che Guevara, Paulo Freire, and the Pedagogy of Revolution*. Boulder, CO: Rowman & Littlefield, 2000.

Slater, J., S. Fain, and C. Rosatto, eds. *The Freirean Legacy: Educating for Social Justice*. New York: Peter Lang Publishing Group, 2002.

Steiner, S., H. Krank, P. McLaren, and R. Bahruth, eds. *Freirean Pedagogy, Praxis, and Possibilities: Projects for the New Millennium*. New York: Falmer Press, 2000.

Index

179

Index

Machismo, 118

Magazines, reading, 152

Marxism, 118

Meaning and interpretation,
54–58

Melo, Tiago de, 74

Milhomem, Gumercindo, 9

"Modernizing discourse," 104

Neoliberal discourse, 20, 104

Newspapers, reading, 152

Obedience, 155–56

Observation, 90

Panic, 50

Parents
ideas about student learning in,
142–45
immoderate behavior in, 82
teachers compared to, 5–9, 28,
62–63

Patience and impatience, 78, 80

*Pedagogy of Hope: A Re-Encounter
with Pedagogy of the Oppressed*
(Freire), 1–2, 4

Permissiveness
problem with, 111–14
students' rejection of, 110

Physics, 137

Piaget, Jean, 45

"Planting sentences," 149

Poetry, 93–95

Politics
education as act of, 111–14, 120,
129

progressive parties and, 20–27
voting power and, 64–67
See also Government

Practice
consciousness of, 137
of democracy, 118–21
of science, 137–38
theory vs., 36–39, 142
thinking and, 139–41, 151

Prepackaged teaching materials,
14–27, 142

Prewriting, 93

Principals, 16

Programming, personal, 125

Progressive parties, 20–27

Progressive teachers, 71–84, 115

Punishment, 109, 147–48

Racism, 119

Radicalism, 104, 114

Rationalism, 92

Reactionary postmodernity, 26

Reading
codification and, 36–38
comprehension and, 34–35,
40–43
cultivating interest in, 76–77
fear of difficulty in, 52–59
relationship of writing to,
44–46
studying as, 33–46
teaching of, 142–47
tools required for, 41
See also Writing

Recording observations, 90

Registration of facts, 107–8

182

Index